JESUS
MAN FOR GOD

Contemporary Issues in Theology

John Toy

Chancellor of York Minster

MOWBRAY
LONDON & OXFORD

First published 1988
by A.R. Mowbray & Co. Ltd,
Saint Thomas House, Becket Street,
Oxford, OX1 1SJ

Typeset by Opus, Oxford
Printed in Great Britain by Billing & Sons Ltd, Worcester

British Library Cataloguing in Publication Data
Toy, John
  Jesus, man for God.
  1. Jesus Christ
  I. Title
  232
  ISBN 0–264–67144–9

For
Mollie
Paul & Katherine

Contents

Preface

The Christian religion is expressed, conveyed and prayed mostly in words; but words change their meanings by being translated into other languages and as they pass from one century into another. So in order to remain true to the revelation given in the past as well as to that which is made known in the present, new words have to be found. That is what contemporary theology is about; it is a task that must be done – Christianity will stultify if it is not – and it is one of the excitements of the twentieth century that it is being done. It is untrue that contemporary theology is mainly negative, concentrating on what cannot be believed rather than on what can and is believed. The truth is that new life is being breathed into old formulas because what is being explored by contemporary theology is the relevance of Christ and his gospel to the world of the twentieth century.

Too often Christian energies are given only to trying to make the past come alive for people – past words, past ideas, past music, past art and past science; that is a worthy task and is congenial to anyone with a respect and love for beauty and good as perceived by former generations. But we must also listen to our own present and try to perceive its own goodnesses and beauties. This work is more tentative and thus more controversial but debate and discussion is a sign of life – to be without it would be stagnation. Debate has gone on all throughout Christian history, and especially in the times of most advance and effectiveness:– the New Testament (eg Paul and James), the age of the Fathers (Arius and Athanasius and the making of the creeds), the middle ages (eg Abelard and Bernard), the Reformation (eg Thomas More and William Tyndale), and the nineteenth century. So it is to be gloried in that there is so much debate and discussion today. We have nothing to fear from rigorous inquiry because we think that truth can only confirm the real gospel of Jesus, who we believe to be the Way, the Truth and the Life. If any of our understanding of the gospel turns out to be untrue or unnecessary, we must have the courage to do without it. We must not suppose we have always possessed the full truth so that we cannot give up or change anything; the Holy Spirit is given to us to *lead us into truth*, into Jesus and through him to God (see *John 16.13*).

Jesus, we believe, was and is God's Man — the man, the only man, wholly for God and wholly possessed by God. That is why he is both an example to us of how God's sort of life can be lived on earth and also our representative before God in eternity. This is what the first Christians meant when they acclaimed him as 'Son of God' and 'Lord'. The central part of this book asks what it is that Christians have believed about Jesus and how we can affirm this belief today. It is prefaced by a section looking at three aspects of the Gospel presentation of Jesus that have been most debated in recent years. It is concluded by a section considering the 'shorthand' affirmations of our beliefs which we call the creeds and how we should regard them and use them today.

The lectures out of which this book has come were given by the present Chancellor of York Minster in fulfilment of the duties of his ancient office, defined in the medieval statutes as 'to give lectures in the vicinity of the church'. He acknowledges with gratitude the loyalty and enthusiasm of those who have attended and the help he has received from their percipient questions and comments.

PART 1

What Can We Believe?

1

The Virgin Birth

The conclusions arrived at at the end of this investigation are as follows – I declare them at the outset so that readers can more easily follow the argument:

1. The idea of the Virgin Birth plays a very small part in the structure of New Testament thought, so small indeed that it is possible to believe all the things that the Gospel claims for Jesus without needing to take the Virgin Birth into account.

2. It is difficult to accept unreservedly any of the theories that have been offered to explain the origin of the story; some of the most frequently offered are:

   a) it originates in the memories of Mary and Joseph; they told others about it later on.

   b) the story was created by Christians as a way of explaining to themselves and others how Jesus could be both fully human and fully divine.

   c) it began when the Gospel was first preached to Greek audiences; they needed to think that Jesus had a god for a father if the claim that he was Son of God was to be substantiated.

   d) it began as a vivid way of demonstrating that the Greek text of *Isaiah 7.14* ('a virgin shall conceive and bear a son') had been fulfilled.

I believe that there are considerable difficulties in accepting any of these as the true explanation; and if you come with me now through the texts of the New Testament I hope you will gain a new understanding and thus a new tolerance, a new respect for those who opt in the circumstances *either* for

3

accepting tentatively that Jesus was born of a virgin, that it actually happened, in default of very strong evidence for another origin of the story *or* for accepting that the story was created by Christian faith as a retrospective assumption about what must have happened in a way which we do not now find necessary. I hope that a greater tolerance for other people's views will come from understanding this issue more deeply. I am not really asking for tolerance for the view that says 'all this Virgin Birth stuff is pure superstitious nonsense: Jesus was a man and that's all there is to it'. Nor am I really asking for tolerance for the person who says 'I believe it all – it is in the Bible, so I believe it literally and completely'. I think both those attitudes can only be held by those who are determined to remain in ignorance of the actual evidence that there is in the Bible about what the first Christians believed about God, about Jesus and about themselves. But if you are willing to listen to the Scriptures, and to the thoughts and opinions of those who have studied the issue in the light of all the knowledge that is available, there is a deeper understanding of the issue waiting for you. That is my aim, to mediate something of that to you from the works of many scholars, commentators and theologians.

The major part of our inquiry must be concerned with the New Testament. There is no disputing the fact that the Virgin Birth was immediately accepted by the vast majority of Christians from the beginning of the second century onwards and that it was used as the foundation and proof of all kinds of assertions about Jesus, Mary, mankind and God from then on, some of which we would now equally strongly affirm and some of which we would all wish to disown, as strongly. But the use made of the doctrine of the Virgin Birth after it had been accepted as part of the revealed truths guaranteed by Scripture must not determine our attitude towards the doctrine, either for or against. The fundamental questions must be: 'is it historical?' and, 'does it give expression to a genuine early insight into the nature of Jesus?'. To answer these questions we must concern ourselves with the New Testament itself.

We begin with Paul, whose writings form the earliest strata of the New Testament and who is thus the first witness to what was known and believed about Jesus. It is often commented that Paul does not refer much to the earthly life of Jesus and does not seem to be interested in it or to depend on it for his proclamation of Jesus' significance. But he does refer to it several times in a way relevant to our concern: for him, Jesus' life on earth was 'in the flesh' whereas his significance was declared by God 'in the spirit': *Rom. 8.3* 'God sent his Son in the likeness of sinful flesh' so that the judgement on sin could be passed in the spirit. *Gal. 4.4* declares that God sent his Son 'born of a woman, born under the law', and the intention clearly there is to affirm that the incarnation placed Jesus in the same situation as the human beings he had come to save. The third passage, *Rom. 1.3* is more important because commentators frequently say that Paul is here probably quoting a creed known to the early Christians and that therefore this bit is a witness not only to Paul's own understanding but also to that of his contemporary fellow Christians: God's Son was born according to the flesh of the seed of David, but according to the Spirit declared Son of God by the resurrection. The use of the word seed here, *sperma*, does I think denote real physical descent from David not just notional or legal descent; as in other passages it is the lordship through the power of the spirit – here linked to the resurrection – that is the saving element.

Now Paul also affirms that the Son always was the Son, and did not merely become it at some point in his life, although we must be aware of emphasizing too much the chronological implications of Paul's pre-existence passages[1]. The Son is spoken of as the Image of God in whom all things were created, before time and after time: this state is his by God's decree and does not seem to have anything to do with the way he came to live his earthly life, which throughout is described in terms of humiliation and identification with us.

Paul preaches a very great status for Jesus and he links it primarily with the risen Christ: he does this without recourse to any affirmation that Jesus had a special form of human existence, rather implying ⸱⸱ ᵁt that was like that of any other human being. Are there any indications that Paul knew of a special way in which Jesus could have been born? If we reject 'born of a woman' in *Gal. 4.4* as giving any such hint, as I think we have to do, (of course one is born of a woman, how else could he express it?), then the only possibility is the argument of *Rom. 9.6* that God's salvation comes, not through natural descent but, as often in the Old Testament, through God's overruling of difficulties or impossibilities, as when Sarah produces Isaac. This of course is not a virgin birth in our sense of the word since Abraham is the natural father. Paul does not link it in any way to Christ's birth, but to the way Christians also become children of God by grace not nature. Anthony Hanson[2] commenting on this passage writes:

> It would be reasonable to suggest that Pauline Christology can stand without a strict doctrine of a Virgin Birth for Christ. But inasmuch as the element of birth-with-promise is a marked feature of the birth narratives in both Matthew and Luke, Paul would certainly have understood and sympathized with their aim. Perhaps there is a moral here to be drawn about the possibility of those who do and those who do not accept the historicity of the Virgin Birth of Christ living together in harmony in the Church.

We turn next to John because he is the other major theologian of the New Testament, not because of his date, though even if he is late in the first century, he must represent many early memories. John like Paul has an exalted concept of Jesus as Son of God and Lord: he also sees the Son as come in the flesh but exalted in the power of the Spirit. Again there are no references to any special manner of his birth. Indeed there are two references to Jesus as the 'son of Joseph'[3] and others implying that he came from Nazareth and that his family was well known. There is an intriguing phrase in *8:41* where the Jews retort 'we were not born of prostitution' which seems to reflect a rumour about Jesus' own origins as being in some way discreditable.[4] This is a point we must come back to in connection with the four women in the Matthean genealogy. Then finally there is the phrase in the Prologue[5] where believers are asserted to be sons of God through the action of God himself directly 'not of human stock, not of the will of the flesh, not of the will of a husband'. Now this is clearly about the sonship of Christians not about Christ's own birth, but could there be such a gap in John's thinking between the two and must not the assertions about the sonship of Christians be linked in his mind somehow with the sonship of Jesus? These are only hints, but we are learning now to look below the surface of the gospels, particularly the fourth, and to appreciate that the hint and the enigmatic phrase may be part of the way they work. Several commentators suggest that the phrase 'son of Joseph' and the reference to his coming from Nazareth not Bethlehem are on the mouths of those of little or no faith, and that perhaps the hint is being given that those in the know, or with a fully developed faith, would see that their objections would disappear with fuller knowledge. After all, it is quite probable, if John does come from near the end of the first century, where the majority of scholars still place him, and the infancy narratives had been gradually becoming widely known, that he could make such allusions: but at the best they are only hints and we have to conclude that John does not draw on the Virgin Birth tradition and that all his affirmations about Christ are made independently of it.

We look now at the three synoptic authors, Matthew, Mark and Luke–Acts (exclusive of the two Infancy Narratives). It is significant, that even in the two works whose final versions were prefaced by the Infancy Narratives, there is no reference to the Virgin Birth in the body of the gospels. There is the incident where Jesus' mother and brothers (and in Matthew and Mark, his sisters also) come to look for him. This is not claimed as a hint that there was not a father but simply suggests that Joseph was not at liberty to travel round Galilee at the time, or, more usually, was dead by then. There are references to Jesus as 'the Son of a carpenter'[6] but these are not important as it is natural that this is what Galileans would think. There is the very intriguing passage, preserved in all three synoptics where the argument seems to be that the Messiah is to be David's Lord and not his Son – a relic perhaps from a Galilean tradition about Jesus with no knowledge of any Bethlehem or Davidic connection? More important I think is the fact that Luke nowhere refers to the Virgin Birth in any of the speeches about Jesus throughout the Acts – even in the work whose final version was prefaced by the story of the Annunciation, the proclamations about Jesus to Jews and Gentiles never allude to the manner of his birth – his Sonship depends on other claims and the first Christians, Acts relates, believed in him for other reasons.

Now at last we turn to the Infancy Narratives: both of them agree in a few points even though all else is different – and the differences between them are so great that some commentators say it is foolish to look at them for history. But some history can well be enshrined in texts which are primarily poetic, symbolic or legendary, so we cannot write the matter off like that. The items on which the Infancy Narratives do agree are:

1) that Jesus' descent from David is to be reckoned through Joseph,
2) that Joseph was not the natural father,
3) that this mystery was announced by an angel,
4) that Mary was betrothed to Joseph,
5) the birth was due to the action of the Holy Spirit,
6) the birth took place in Bethlehem.

There seems to be a discrepancy between the first two of these so let us look first at the genealogies: the descent is traced through Joseph, by different routes; they must have first been compiled to show that Jesus the Son of Joseph was of the line of David. When incorporated into narratives asserting the Virgin Birth there were three ways of dealing with them: first, to alter the text; there are signs of this in both Matthew and Luke:- Matthew has several later variants in place of 'Joseph the husband of Mary of whom was born Jesus called the Messiah' asserting Mary's virginity or that they wre only betrothed; Luke has the phrase 'as was supposed', strongly suggesting an insertion although no version omits it. The second way to reconcile the two is to suggest (against the text) that the genealogy of Luke is that of Mary not Joseph, thus preserving a physical descent from David even if Joseph was not the father: this of course is the medieval tradition represented for example in the Jesse windows and in many carols. The third way to cope, and this is common to many commentaries, is to suggest that since Joseph by his betrothal to Mary was the legal father then Jesus had the status of a son of David even if he was not physically one. I think we must accept that this was the sense in which the final editors of Matthew and Luke meant us to understand it, if they actually did give the matter any thought.

Now Matthew's genealogy has a regular pattern which suggests it is making a point about the scheme worked by God in his plan for the salvation of the nations, from Abraham to David, from David to the exile, and from the exile to Jesus. And it includes, not usual in Jewish genealogies, the names of five women: Tamar, Rahab, Ruth, Bathsheba, called simply her belonging to Uriah, and Mary. Why? Not famous women because Sarah and Rebecca would be there:

 i) perhaps because they were exalted in Jewish traditions as particularly righteous and zealous for the welfare of Israel,

 ii) perhaps because they are thought of as aliens prefiguring the Saviour of the Gentiles as well as of the Jews,

iii) but it could be because all five were suspected in their time of adultery and their inclusion shows how the purposes of God can overrule the weaknesses of men. The rumour that Jesus had been conceived illegitimately – either by an unknown man or by Joseph before their formal marriage, could be hinted at here.

The point is that it is God's power that produces the Saviour; no contribution of man is needed and God can and does use the weakest of vessels to do His work on the earth. Here we are getting close not only to the motive for putting the four women into the genealogy but also to the motive of the Virgin Birth narrative as well. All the way through the story of salvation, God has acted in spite of the weakness and the sin of his chosen servants down the ages, overcoming impossibilities, objections and lack of faith, signalling these often by the message of an angel which communicates the favour of God and the greatness of the child to be produced. It is the activity of the Holy Spirit of God that enables birth to take place, not, in the many examples in the Old Testament, in spite of the lack of sexual intercourse but in spite of impotency; virgin birth in the strict sense of the miraculous impregnation of a *virgo intacta* does not occur anywhere in the Old Testament. Outside in the non-Jewish world of course examples abound because, outside Judaism, Sonship of God was not a status conferred by God to perform a function and in response to faith and obedience, but could only be thought of physically: to have your claim to be a Son of God accepted in the pagan world you really ought to have had a god as father.

Let us now turn to the Lukan infancy narrative, or to be precise, to the Annunciation account, for there is no reference to the Virgin Birth in the Nativity narrative; there Mary and Joseph are referred to as Jesus' parents (2.27) and as his father and mother (2.33). Luke offers two parallel accounts of a divine assisted birth: Zacharias is told by an angel that in spite of his and Elizabeth's impotency and age there will be a child and its name and function is outlined. Zacharias questions the possibility of a child, is rebuked for lack of faith: Elizabeth knows she is pregnant and says 'The Lord has done this to me in the days in which he has looked upon me' (1.25). This of course is not a virgin birth if virgin means a girl who has not had sexual intercourse: but Geza Vermes[7] has pointed out that in Jewish usage the word also means a girl who has not reached puberty and is, in Philo, used for a matron who has passed the menopause. This warns us that in Jewish usage the term 'virgin' is not as precise as we would think, and could cover various ways of not normally being able to conceive. In the second passage Mary is told by an angel that she will have a child and its name and functions are outlined. Mary says

'How shall this be seeing I know not a man?' This too can be taken as an objection, a questioning, and the process is more fully explained in much the same way as Elizabeth: 'The Holy Spirit will come upon you and the power of the Most High will overshadow you'.[8]

In a passage that does have such strong Old Testament overtones, the strangest part is not really the birth to a girl who is only betrothed, but the very un-Jewish sound to the last part of verse 35 'Wherefore that which is to be born shall be called holy, a Son of God': the virginal conception seems to be necessary to make the title Son of God possible. Some commentators see this as the origin of the idea, grafted here on to a passage that originates in the Old Testament world of miraculous, but not virgin, births. In his commentary on the Gospel, Leaney,[9] thinks that there are at least three different traditions that have been brought together in these two chapters:

1) that Mary conceived virginally, with no reference to being betrothed,
2) that Mary was divinely promised that she would be the Mother of the Messiah after her marriage to Joseph to whom she was betrothed, and
3) that she conceived during her betrothal by cohabitation with Joseph.

Leaney is certainly not alone in thinking that the Lukan narratives are rather a mixture of different ideas and traditions, one of which is clearly that Jesus was born of a virgin. Note that Luke makes no reference or allusion to *Isaiah 7.14*.

By contrast, the Annunciation in Matthew is much less complicated. There the Virgin Birth is stated clearly to Joseph and is the central point of the story. Like all the component parts of Matthew's opening chapters it is explained as fulfilling a text of Scripture – in this case the Greek text of *Isaiah 7.14*, a *parthenos* shall conceive and bear a son. Some commentators claim that the Virgin Birth in Matthew is thus a deduction from the text of Isaiah – 'if the Scripture says that, it must have been so': others claim that Matthew must have the idea already and only searches around for texts to attach to it. In this case then the idea of the Virgin Birth in Matthew is not created by the Isaiah passage and Matthew has received it independently.

Having looked at the New Testament, then how can we attempt to answer the two questions we posed ourselves. First, does the Virgin Birth correspond to something that actually happened, is it historical? There is only one possible answer, we cannot know. The only evidence that the New Testament provides is of such a marginal character that a firm answer cannot be given. R.E.Brown writes 'while Matthew and Luke apparently accepted the virginal conception as historical, we cannot be certain where they got their information on this point'. The older theories that all information in Luke's Infancy Narrative came straight from Mary's side of the family, while Matthew's information came from Joseph's side, is no longer tenable in modern exegesis – even though family origins for some information cannot be *a priori* excluded. Consequently we must face the possibility that in good faith the evangelists have taken over an earlier belief in virginal conception that does not have an authentic historical basis. Hendrickx who quotes this[10] says that he speaks for the vast majority of Catholic exegetes, and we would add for non-Catholic ones as well. But this of course does not mean that it is definitely not historical: it *could* be, but there is no way of being sure since it also could have originated in a rabbinic style midrash, (improving meditation) over *Isaiah 7.14* or in the desire to convince Gentiles that Jesus was a divine being, a Son of God; or it could have originated in the affirmation that God acted finally and decisively in human history by sending his Son and this was a way of affirming Jesus' eschatological and God-given character. This leads us to give some attention to what the doctrinal significance of the doctrine looks like now in the 20th century and how we can react to its inclusion in the Apostles' and Nicene Creeds.

Once the New Testament Scriptures became fixed, all Christians accepted the Virgin Birth: it played no particular part in the great Christological controversies since all the participants, heretics and orthodox, affirmed it. It seemed to them that it could be a useful way of explaining how Jesus could be both God and man since ancient man generally held to a view of human generation, (*now known to be false*), that the female supplies the matter of humanity while the male supplies the active principle of generation.[11] Thus Mary was thought to supply the complete human nature and the Holy Spirit gave the divine nature or soul.

Here lies the great difficulty that faces 20th century Christians with this doctrine. We now know that human nature must be derived from both parents since the heredity (the genes) of both are essential and that a Jesus from only one parent (apart from the fact that a human with only female genes must be a female) is a diminished human being, not a complete human being, and certainly not like us in everything. Whereas it is fully appreciated that in ancient times 'born of the Virgin Mary' was hailed as a guarantee of Jesus' humanity against the tendencies of those who wanted to see him just as a God on earth, now it has the opposite effect in denying Jesus a natural procreation like ours and thus reducing the wonder of the Incarnation not enhancing it. Emil Brunner[12] saw this as long ago as 1934 and J.A.T.Robinson[13] gave forceful expression to it more recently.

The other great difficulty that 20th century Christians have with the doctrine of the Virgin Birth is the way it has been associated through centuries of theological argument and poetry with Jesus' sinlessness, as if being a virgin was somehow more pure than being a married woman and so Jesus was started off on the path of sinlessness by not being procreated by the degrading act of sexual intercourse and having as his only human parent a 'pure virgin'. This point of view was of course given a great impetus by the argument fostered by St Augustine that the guilt of original sin was passed down from Adam by the sexual act so that if a break was to be made and a sinless human being created then it had to be miraculous and not by the normal means of human procreation. The same idea led to the theory, against the evidence of the New Testament, of the perpetual virginity of

Mary (the 'ever virgin' of ancient prayers and hymns) and even further extravagances such as the Immaculate Conception. Now I take it for granted that we must reject all this and give Jesus the full glory for his sinlessness, as the Epistle to the Hebrews does, that he was tempted at all points as we are and yet without sin. The sinlessness lay not in *the nature he was provided with* from birth but in his own *obedience to his Father's will* in all things, even to the death on the cross.

But because we reject some of the uses that Christians have made of the idea of the Virgin Birth of Christ, we need not feel obliged to reject the doctrine itself, especially, as I hope I have shown, there is a remote possibility that there was something strange and unusual and perhaps even shocking about the way Jesus was born and because it stands in the creeds intended to be an affirmation of Jesus' full humanity. It is because of this that Pannenberg[14] says Christians can still confess this part of the creed —

> in worship without abandoning truthfulness. The repetition of a confession of the church is certainly something different from the faith of an individual. Whoever joins in the confession of the church confesses the unity of Christianity through time by placing himself in the context of the intention expressed in the formulations even where the mode of expression must be perceived as inappropriate.

That is why it is perfectly appropriate to join in the words of the creed 'born of the Virgin Mary' even if one inclines to the view that it was the theological, sociological and biological issues of the age rather than actual historicity that created the stories. But the bishops of the Church of England, when they were called upon to pronounce on this issue, insisted that in their corporate view the hints in other parts of the New Testament were sufficient to make the historicity of the Virgin Birth an option which one could hold 'with full intellectual integrity' and they asserted that an important theological point was being made by the traditional doctrine 'that in Christ God has taken the initiative for our salvation by uniting our human nature with himself, so bringing into being a new humanity'.[15]

I think Emil Brunner put it well in *The Mediator*:[16]

> It is not my desire to enter into controversy about the doctrine: rather I would here express my indifference to this as to all other attempts to explain the miracle of the Incarnation. We simply stand amazed before the Fact itself without thinking it necessary to combine with this certain inquisitive biological ideas.

Let us acknowledge then the many different ways that Christians have tried to understand and proclaim the Incarnation: some are more suitable to the knowledge and experience of one age than to another: some are more eloquent to one individual's understanding, than to another's: but it is the permanent and universal significance of Jesus that they are all concerned with, and if we hold to that, we shall be united in what matters and God in His good and plentiful time will take care of the various ways of expressing it.

2

The Nature Miracles of Jesus

The Virgin Birth and the Resurrection are associated with Christmas and Easter, they concern the beginning and end of Christ's life and feature in the creeds. The miracles performed by Jesus during his public ministry, on the other hand, can seem very much of a side-issue, a detail of the Jesus-tradition towards which one does not have to take up a stance because few people regard acceptance of these events as being of the essence of Christianity. Yet in many ways the issues raised by Jesus' miracles underlie the other two – did God do extraordinary things in and through Jesus of Nazareth and if so why? Do the claims that Christians make for Jesus include, or even depend upon, his ability to bypass the observed 'laws' of nature; did he choose to exercise those powers, and what does it mean for us that he did or did not? How do we respond to reports from the 1st century AD about miraculous happenings in those far off times?

We acknowledge first of all that for many Christians from almost the beginning of Christianity up to now, the miracles of Jesus have been seen as evidence that he was God's Son, proofs of his divinity and thus part of the Church's equipment for creating faith in him.

This view depends of course on denying or minimizing similar miraculous happenings reported of other heroes and leaders and in other religions but its appeal is simple and forceful: 'If he did things which only the Creator of the world can do, his teachings must be right and we must put our faith in him'. The obverse of this is equally clear: 'since we believe Jesus to have been the unique Son of God, through whom all things were made, then he could be expected to be able to heal diseases, quell storms, raise the dead and change water into wine and we have no difficulty in accepting the witness of those who said they saw him do these things. A unique person can do unique things. That's all there is to it'. Now there are two things to note about this position: the first is the strength of this attitude in the minds of many ordinary believers up to and including the present time: a general rejection of the miraculous for themselves, for their own time, for other heroes and leaders but an acceptance of the miracles of Jesus, 'because he was God'. The second thing to note is that all exponents of the New Testament in this century, conservative and radical, Catholic and Protestant, agree that *that is not why any of the New Testament writers tell us about the miracles*: it is not *as miracles* that they are significant or are seen as significant: it is the content of them, *what* is done, that matters and that carries a message for hearers of the Gospel.

We must come back to that after we have acknowledged a second fact: for many people from the beginning of Christianity, and particularly from the 17th century up to now, the miracles of Jesus have been the most enormous barrier to total acceptance of him and of Christianity. Whereas Jesus comes across the centuries compelling in his message about God, in his stand for truth and the strength of his spirit and example, the character of wonder-worker and magician seems to be part of the furniture of primitive ages that should now be discarded. Whereas Jesus refused to give signs, his followers cluttered up the Gospel with the stories, which the piety of those centuries demanded, but which in the light of modern knowledge, became hinderances rather than helps to faith.

We must acknowledge the strength of this attitude in the minds of many ordinary members of our congregations up to and including the present time. I have heard many a sermon where a naturalistic explanation of a miracle of Jesus (e.g. the miracle of the feeding of the 5,000 as an initiatory act of sharing the boy's meal, giving the lead to hundreds of others sharing their meal; or walking on the water being really walking on a shallow spit of sand) has been offered hesitantly or apologetically as a way of making it more possible to accept the passage being expounded and as presenting Jesus as more believable, more able to help people like us than if he was a performer of wonders.

So with these two rather contrasting attitudes to the miracles of Jesus in our minds, let us turn to the New Testament where most of our inquiry is to be pursued. Immediately we are struck by a difference from our investigation of the Virgin Birth: whereas we looked through the New Testament and found only two passages clearly mentioning the Virgin Birth of Jesus, all four gospels narrate quite freely many miracles performed by Jesus during his public ministry, so we obviously have here a feature of the proclamation of Jesus from the earliest times. Nevertheless, it is interesting to note that the vast majority of the miracles are in the Markan material and distributed very heavily towards the front of his gospel; it is because Matthew and Luke use Mark extensively that they have these miracles too, but there are very few in their own distinctive bits or in the long sections that Matthew and Luke have in common which we call Q.[17] John you remember says that many miracles were done but he chooses just a few to draw out their significance for his readers.[18]

Much of what we must say concerns all the miracles of Jesus but we concentrate on the nature miracles because they have difficulties of their own. Most of the miracles are healings, either exorcisms or healing physical diseases or deformities or, most dramatic of all, raisings from the dead. The latter deserve special consideration which cannot be given here, but the healings have never caused quite the same difficulties as they are more obviously compassionate acts and the modern mind can more easily conceive of ways in which the presence of someone like Jesus could powerfully affect both mind and hence the body of sufferers brought before him; but the nature miracles are more difficult to many because matter rather than persons are involved and some of them are very weak in the compassionate element. What are the nature miracles? Seven are usually listed: the walking on the water, the stilling of the storm, the great catch of fish, the water into wine, the feeding of the 5,000, the coin in the fish's mouth and the withered fig tree, but we must recognize that this distinction is not one which can be made by the New Testament itself. In the ancient world the power of spirits was everywhere apparent and the stilling of the storm would have counted as an exorcism, casting out the demons of chaos, for the whole of nature was seen as animate and responsive to authority.

Here an effort of imagination is necessary to understand the world in which these writings were created; if we want to understand what is being told us about Jesus we have got to attune our ears to hear the New Testament writers talking their language – they do not talk in ours and the sort of world they are talking about is not in all respects the one we know and live in. When we have heard what they are telling us about Jesus in their world, then we must respond to the same Jesus in terms of our world and our situation; nothing can protect us from having to do that but we have the promise of the Spirit of God to aid us.

The miracle tradition in the gospels has its origin in the memory of those who knew Jesus' ministry in Galilee: there the universal popular view accepted that the world was full of spirits and powers – good, bad and indifferent; men and women could be possessed by these powers and a great many strange things happened all the time, but Jesus came doing not just wonders and signs, but particular kinds of wonders and signs that meant something, that declared a message about what God was doing in and through him. Indeed to see them just as wonders, and simply to marvel *that* they were done, was *to fail to understand*, to see but not perceive, to remain on the outside: but to see *what* was being done, to recognize that if the expected signs of the coming of the kingdom were being effected then the final opportunity for repentance and faith was at hand or, in the later more refined presentation of the issue represented strongly in the fourth Gospel, to recognize that what was being done proclaimed the doer of these things to be God's Son and word, this brought you to the inside as one who had got the message and responded appropriately.

All four evangelists present Jesus as one who brought in a foretaste of God's kingdom *not only in what he said but also in what he did* and that contact with Jesus so often resulted – for those who had eyes to see, not everyone; they were always private or semi-private occasions, never public – in healing, restoration, encouragement. There must have been in Jesus such a concentration of God's power and spirit, or as John Macquarrie calls it in his discussion of miracle, such a 'focussing'[19] of power that unexpected, uncharted, unusual, not-yet-understood phenomena could have occurred. I do not think we are now able to see this only in terms of mind over matter in the human body but have to be prepared to grant the possibility of natural miracles as well in principle – for is not modern physics more ready than most other disciplines to accept the extremely unlikely or even the previously impossible, particularly in situations of the release of great power? Schillebeeckx[20] argues in twenty pages of great interest on the gospel miracles that the causing of exceptionally strange and startling events is a necessary supposition about Jesus of Nazareth to account for the extreme reaction to him that the historical sources witness to: some people said that he was of the devil and ought to be silenced immediately: others that he was of God and is to be followed even at cost: even the apathetic multitude were interested enough in him to flock to see him. This very fact says Schillebeeckx is the most important datum in the whole miracle question. Although the miracle tradition is primarily from the memories of the ordinary country folk in Galilee, and although in the gospels the historic and the kerygmatic are inextricably tangled, we cannot and must not rule out the historic.

If we admit it in principle then we go to each of the individual miracles ready to accept that it *could* have happened, unless there are things in the texts that signal to us that that particular story had its origin rather more obviously in proclamation or piety. Acceptance that Jesus could have been the cause of miracles does not mean for anyone who takes the New Testament seriously, automatic acceptance that all the miracles happened as narrated. We must listen to the clues that the New Testament itself gives us, and to what we know about the world of the first century AD We must recognise that there were strong motives, already visible in the New Testament writings, but mainly typical of the developing Christian piety of the 2nd and 3rd centuries AD to multiply miracles, producing doublets, increasing the numbers of persons or objects involved, signalling key incidents with a miracle, developing Old Testament parallels by creating incidents with a miracle, developing Old Testament parallels and generalizing from the traditions of certain incidents about the frequency of miracles overall. Some of you will know the apocryphal gospels, with their stories of Jesus as a boy wreaking havoc among people who rebuked or offended him, finding lost goods, turning models into real animals, helping Joseph out of a difficulty in the carpenter's shop, and bringing the dead back to life: these stories go back to at least the second century AD From the pagan world of the time we have numerous miracle stories of religious and folk heroes, many of them paralleling the type of thing told about Jesus. Now it is often remarked that the New Testament narratives owe more to the Old Testament miracles than to pagan models and that there is a reticence and delicacy about the way the Gospels handle miracles that distinguishes them from these later pious stories. This is undoubtedly true, yet we must be careful: the motive is there, to exalt Jesus as at least as good as anyone else and the readiness to believe in miracles was there.

We look now at the seven traditional nature miracles of Jesus, in the light of what commentators say about them.

The first is the *miraculous catch of fish*[21] told by Luke as an incident on the lake of Galilee near the beginning of his public ministry and by John[22] as a resurrection event in the same place. There are three variants on the traditional interpretation – that these are two separate miraculous events, which is to be found in some commentaries. One is that this was not meant to be a miracle, just a coincidence or the result of Jesus standing on the shore being able to see where the fish were. The second is that this is a resurrection story, as John has it, and that Luke or his source has attached it wrongly to the saying about 'fishers of men' at the call of the disciples: there are some features about the Lukan version, particularly Peter's 'Depart from me for I am a sinful man O Lord'[23] that could fit better into the latter context. The third variant is to say with John Marsh[24] and others that we can see here how in the telling of the gospel story over the years it gets elaborated: starting with the Markan story, which Matthew has, about the four fishermen who are called by Jesus in the midst of their work and told they will become fishers of men, this is illustrated by Luke with a story that shows that under Jesus' instruction a disciple really does begin to get results and John adds to this the point that under the risen power of Christ, not just Peter and his companions but all his followers can bring in the harvest of the gospel: the 153 fish being all the known kinds of fish in the ancient world and thus representing all the peoples of the earth. The symbolism is particularly strong in the way the story is told in John, as Hoskyns and Davey[24] emphasize and I for one must conclude that its claims to be an actual event are not as strong as many other miracles.

Second is the *stilling of the storm* in Mark, Matthew and Luke.[26] This is perhaps the most straightforward of this group: told in similar words in the three synoptic gospels, Mark with a stress on it as a declaration by Jesus of the power of the creator God working through Jesus to quell chaos, and by Matthew with a characteristic stress on Jesus' power to help his disciples in all their troubles. The Old Testament motifs are strong and several commentators think that they may have created the story as a claim that the Spirit working through Jesus was able to conquer all others: others affirm that some incident memorable to those present must lie behind the story, and I incline to think they are right.

Third, we have the *feeding of the multitudes*:[27] unique of all the miracle stories in appearing in all four gospels and twice in Matthew and Mark, very similar stories in all six accounts. Its popularity among the traditions of the early church must be because of its association with the service of the breaking of bread, which is the focus point where the language in all six accounts becomes exactly the same and is the context that John clearly puts the story in his following discourse. But many different symbolisms converge in the way this story is told: it recalls Moses who fed the wilting Israelites with bread from heaven,[28] it recalls Elijah and Elisha[29] who made twenty barley loaves feed a hundred men and still there was something over and it affirms therefore that Jesus does all that Moses and Elijah did and more: indeed it comes so close to those Old Testament stories that it could have originated in eucharistic expositions on these texts as applied to Jesus. But as an act of compassion and as a symbolic anticipation of the messianic banquet, I can see it as something done by Jesus and remembered with awe and reverence by those few who knew what was happening: nowhere is it told just as a miracle story – it is the meaning that dominates completely and thus it cannot have been created as a miracle story – it must have arisen from the tradition either as a remembered incident heavy with meaning and symbolism or as having its origin in the proclamation of Jesus as provider. Here again, I think the weight and nature of the evidence just favours an original incident but the commentators are very divided over this.

Fourth, we have the *walking on the water*[30] which comes immediately after the feeding of the five thousand in Mark, Matthew and John. Many commentators are not convinced that this is meant to be a miracle at all. The phrase 'on the sea' could equally well be translated 'by the sea' and the disciples reassured by seeing Jesus. It could be intended to be a vision of the disciples, not a physical reality. It relates to the language of *Job 9.8 and 11* 'It is God who treads on the crests of the waves: he passes by me and I do not see him', but the similarity is not strong enough to say that the story originates in exposition of those verses. The fact that it is firmly attached to the feeding incident speaks in favour of memory of an incident and inclines many commentators to come down hesitantly on the side of an historic origin although C.F.D.Moule[31] remarks, as he does with most of the nature miracles, 'the question is not could God have done this through Jesus, but would he?'

Fifth, there is the *coin in the fish's mouth*[32] with which Peter pays the temple tax. 'No reader at that time would have taken the passage literally' declares Schillebeeckx[33] who accepts the historicity of most miracles; even conservative-evangelical commentators gulp at this one, suggesting perhaps that it was only meant to report a coincidence not a miracle. 'Clearly a fable', say most commentators and I certainly think one must reject it as likely to be unhistorical: could Jesus have been so trivial as actually to do this? It is surely the same sort of miracle as those in the apocryphal gospels; it is not surprising that a few of these could have got into the earlier gospels.

Sixth, there is *the fig tree which withered up when cursed by Jesus*[34] at the time he cleansed the temple in the last days in Jerusalem. A story in both Mark and Matthew; again rather unedifying if it was meant to be a miracle: there has clearly been some confusion as to whether it is an autumn story when figs would be expected or a passover time story when figs could not be on the tree. Most commentators say this must have been a parable by Jesus, pointing out a barren fig tree, which has got turned into a miracle during its many retellings. Tasker[35] says Jesus saw it was dying and foretold its death, thus getting rid of the cursing element, but preserving the miraculous by making it die quickly in a day or two. But this does nothing to help the conjuring trick element that makes it so difficult to fit doing a thing like this just to illustrate a point with the character of Jesus we get from everywhere else in the gospels. A subjective judgement maybe, but it is one most commentators make.

Seventh, and last, we come to the *changing of water into wine*[36] at the marriage of Cana placed by John as the first of the signs done by Jesus and not included in the other gospels. It is clear to all commentators that it is the symbolism of this story that is important: indeed it is so important to John that he emphasizes the details in such a way that he seems to be signalling that the symbolism has taken over any remains of historicity. Jesus turns the water of Judaism into the wine of the kingdom of God and with such effect as to surpass any previous feasts. Each store jar holds 20 gallons, they are filled up to the brim, and a village wedding where the guests had already well drunk was suddenly provided with 120 gallons more. Now whatever the original situation was, John is clearly more interested in the symbolism: this is not the sort of trick Jesus would have done just like that and almost all commentators agree. Further light is thrown by a passage from Philo, which must have been written before the earliest possible date for the Fourth Gospel, expounding the Melchizedek passage in Genesis 14 as being about the Word, the Logos, who when he comes 'will bring wine instead of water . . . and will cheer your souls with unmixed wine in order that they may be wholly occupied in a divine intoxication'. This is exactly the same point as St John is making about Jesus and it will not do, as Hoskyns & Davey[37] do, to dismiss it as irrelevant. But I do not think that John could develop the symbolism in the way he does unless he thought he was handling something that actually happened, even though he felt free here, as he did in other places, to change the details of the story to bring out insights into who Jesus was that to him, were much more important and significant even than the question of exactly what happened at Cana in Galilee.

In conclusion: the gospels ask us to put our faith in a way of life taught and lived by one who authenticated himself to men and women of his own time in ways that they were able to accept. In the New Testament they offer their own convictions and insights to us but the Church has never insisted that we should believe for the same reasons that they did: what matters is that we share their faith *in* Jesus as the Way, the Truth and the Life and their belief *that* he did certain things is not the faith that saves.

3

The Resurrection of Christ

No one would deny that when we consider the resurrection of Christ we are very near the heart of the Christian Faith; but it is important to be very accurate here: what is the heart of the Christian Faith is an assertion, a confession and the essence of the confession is that in spite of all that man did to Jesus by denying him, abandoning him and crucifying him, he may still be hailed as Lord, as one who rightly spoke of God and showed us what the life of faith amounts to; certainly this confession is interpretation, and the words vary somewhat according to which of the witnesses you are listening to: Paul, John, Mark, Luke, Matthew or one of the others; the interpretation varies but the central thing is that what they are interpreting is an event in history. All are agreed that what they are talking about is something that has happened, something that God has done in the world that shows that He is righteous. He has declared his righteousness by this act. This invites comparison with the great acts of interpreted history from Israel's past, the Exodus, the Conquest of Canaan, the Exile and return from exile and the Maccabean triumph after the persecutions of Antiochus; all these, say the Christians, have been overshadowed now by this new act of God with Jesus. The heart of the Christian Faith then is not the resurrection, exaltation, vindication, ascension or the continuous presence of Jesus as such, for all these are words to try to clarify the significance of what happened; the heart of the faith is the event – it happened – and the interpretations that see this event as world-shattering and relevant to everyone; it is the one great miracle where the facts of Jesus turn into the interpretation of them. It is the very focus point of the relationship between history and Christian faith.

This event burst into the experience of puzzled and dis-spirited disciples, and changed in a very short time their manner of regarding Jesus and responding to him. This change is an undisputed fact of history; while the explanation of what caused this change may well be a matter of interpretation – historians may not always agree on it – but the nature of the change must be recognized from the first; and proper respect must be paid to the Christian claim that because the event is unique and outside previous human experience it cannot be fully explained in familiar terms and categories. There must at least be a readiness to admit that something new has occurred. But that does not mean that either the first disciples or we can create entirely new words to interpret this event, even if we have a suspicion that it may have this unique character. The words we use are given to us by past human experience, reflection and aspirations. That applies to the words the first disciples used to themselves, in their first sermons and eventually in their New Testament writings, words like 'risen', 'raised', 'ascended', 'exalted', 'declared Son of God', 'sitting at God's right hand', 'gone to the Father', 'made Lord and Christ' and many others; all these words and phrases have a pre-history and we can expect to get some understanding of what the first apostles meant by looking at the antecedents of the words they chose to use.

The Language to Hand

God and God alone could bring life out of death; but the Jew of classic times did not expect God to do this in the ordinary course of events. Life went out of you when you died, you gave back to God the spirit of life-giving breath that He had given you and you declined into the lifeless state of existence known as Sheol-somewhat misleadingly translated 'hell' in some of the old translations – a pale shadow-like state where the only life that you had was not yours but what you passed on to your descendents; hence the importance of being married for if you had no children you had no life of any kind. But from the Exile onwards, under the pressure of the individualization of religion and the influence of the beliefs of other nations, the notion of personal survival after death became familiar. The power of God to raise the dead and give them back the breath of life they had forfeited had always been acknowledged and the hopes of the exiles used this image for national revival (the dry bones passage of *Ezekiel 37* for example) and later as an apocalyptic expectation for individual Israelites (*Daniel 12.1*). A great impetus was given by the traumas of the Maccabean revolt and all the faithful Jews who then gave their lives in defence of God's law; God would surely raise up these righteous souls from the death so unjustly and ignominiously inflicted on them so that they could share with those left alive in the glories of the kingdom of God, to which they had witnessed so bravely and sacrificially.

Although in Jesus' lifetime, the Sadducees held out against the notion that resurrection either to rewards or punishments was to be expected when God brought in his kingdom – they did this because as conservative fundamentalists they would not accept an idea that could not be proved from holy Scripture, particularly an idea that was of comparatively recent origin and owed something to the beliefs of Gentile unbelievers – the Pharisees and the Jewish population generally accepted this idea. Jesus told stories that presupposed this idea, such as the parable of the sheep and goats in *Matt 25.31* and the parable of Dives and Lazarus in *Luke 16.19*, and when he was challenged about his own opinion when the Sadducees asked about the woman who had had seven husbands, his reply (*Mark 12.26*) assumes that there will be a resurrection; at the very least he is accepting what was the popular belief and is certainly not supporting the Saducees in their reluctance to accept the idea.

It is important to recognise that the Jew who lived in the first century AD was in a cultural whirlpool; there were all kinds of ideas going around about the future and much overlapping. Teachers often try to make a rigid distinction between *resurrection of the body* as a 'genuine' Jewish idea **that takes the unity of soul, mind and body seriously and *the*** *immortality of the soul* as a fundamentally Greek idea built upon the notion of the soul imprisoned in vile flesh which is the cause of its pollution and from which it flees at death. The distinction is not invalid conceptually but it must not be urged as operable in the first century AD The New Testament itself witnesses to how easily both ideas lived together in Christian thought, and so they did in the Jewish world out of which the gospel sprang. *4 Ezra* for example is a kind of compendium of eschatological and apocalyptic ideas[38] in which rising to life again, ascending to a new world, going to heaven in clouds of glory, being restored to life on this earth all feature. Other works combine immortality with exaltation and make little mention of resurrection.

Nevertheless, the specific question 'What then will it be like for us; what body will we have?' posed a problem for the Jew. All his tradition urged him not to go straight for the normal Hellenistic answer and say simply that no body was involved at all, since that was left behind to putrify in the earth; he could not just talk like that because his tradition had taught him that God had made the whole of man, and that all aspects went to make up the person so that you could not have a real, whole man without brain, mind, heart, emotions, spirit and soul to say nothing of flesh and bone, blood and muscle. The complication facing the Jew was that, whereas he wanted to affirm that all this was resurrected – so that the real, whole individual could be seen to be alive again and not just a part, shadow or aspect of him, he also wanted to affirm that it was not a question of resuscitation to the old kind of life again; the whole point of the great act of God in righteous judgement was that it would be a renewal of the earth and a glorious re-creation. On the one hand the body had to be *continuous* with the old but on the other hand it had also to be *discontinuous* with it. This is one of the reasons for the variety of imagery and metaphor that we find in the first century world, a variety that sometimes strikes the modern systematizing mind as simply confusing and imprecise. Alternatively it can lead to a chronological, timetabling treatment of the matter according to which things happen in *two stages*; first, a body continuous with the old is raised up that goes on living on the earth and then secondly another event occurs which transforms everything so that the body becomes discontinuous.

You can see why these expectations about the nature of the resurrection body have direct relevance for our understanding of the language which the New Testament preachers and writers chose to use. The apparent ambivalence about the nature of the body of Jesus (eg passing through doors yet Thomas is invited to touch: appearing and disappearing yet he eats food to show he is not a ghost) is not caused by the inventiveness of the different evangelists but by the necessity to do justice to the continuity and the discontinuity of the risen body. And the framework adopted by St Luke of a two-stage process, which is where our church year comes from with Easter as a feast to celebrate the continuity of Jesus' body and then, 40 days later, Ascension to celebrate its discontinuity, can immediately be seen not just as history – this is how it actually was – but as fitting in to one of the expected scenarios of how it would be at the end. There is a most illuminating parallel to Luke in a first century AD Jewish Apocalypse that was probably written at almost exactly the same time as Luke's gospel or a little after, that was much used and valued by Christians for many centuries: *2 Baruch*. Baruch asks the question:

> What kind of life will be given to those who see your day? What kind of glory will they possess after such happenings? Will they re-assume their present appearance?

and he gets the answer:

> The earth shall assuredly restore the dead as it has received them, for then it will be necessary to show to those who are alive that the dead have come back to life, and when they have severally recognized those whom they know then shall judgement grow strong and the things spoken of before will come about . . . and the

splendour of those who have been justified shall be glorified in changes, and they shall be transformed into the splendour of angels (*2 Baruch 50.2–4*)

Here bodily resurrection is a prelude to the real glorification of the elect and it performs a secondary function, to persuade those still left on the earth that it really is a resurrection of those whom they knew; here it is primarily a matter of individuals, no longer the corporate event of the earlier Judaism; then comes the actual eschatological event when the righteous are transformed and become like the angels (compare Jesus' phrase in *Mark 12.25*).

None of these considerations diminishes the importance of what God did with Jesus after the crucifixion; but they show that the disciples did not invent a new language to communicate it – how could they anyway, when the essence of communication is to make use of words and ideas that are already familiar even when communicating something new; the newness lies in the combination of ideas and in the implications seen that have not been seen before. Neither Jesus himself nor his disciples lived in a vacuum or could be uninfluenced by the world in which they grew up; there were certain sets of ideas around in their world about what God would do at the last day, and whatever they said and did would inevitably be related to these ideas. Let us turn to look at some of the crucial passages.

The Earliest Evidence for Easter Language

Probably the earliest evidence for belief in the resurrection of Jesus is to be found in Paul's letters, the earliest writings in the New Testament, where he is most likely quoting some credal statements that pre-date his letters. In *1 Cor. 15.3–8* we have:

> that Christ died for our sins, according to the Scriptures; that he was buried; and that he was raised to life on the third day, in accordance with the Scriptures; that he appeared first to Cephas and secondly to the Twelve. Next he appeared to more than five hundred of the

> brothers at the same time, most of whom are still alive,
> though some have died; then he appeared to James, and
> then to all the apostles; and last of all he appeared to me
> too.

By the last sentence we have certainly left the credal statement
and are listening to an addition made by Paul himself; the rest
sounds as if it is a carefully compiled chronological list of
appearances which has been passed on to Paul, *viz* 1) to
Cephas 2) to the Twelve 3) to the 500 4) to James and 5) to all
the apostles; although it must be noted that some see only the
first two belonging to the formula because, like the preceding
phrases, they are prefaced with 'that'. Our first attention,
however, must be given to the part that is clearly credal in
form 1) died for our sins 2) was buried 3) raised to life on the
third day, and 4) appearance to Cephas and the Twelve, with
the first and third having the comment, 'according to the
Scriptures', i.e. this is part of God's long-laid and long-ago-
declared plan of salvation for Israel and through Israel to the
world. This assertion may refer generally to the dying and the
being raised, or more particularly to the 'for our sins' and to
the 'on the third day', but, whichever it is, this phrase is
important as showing the desire to link the Easter event with
the fulfilment of the Scriptures.

Why 'he was buried'? In later ages this was seen as
emphasizing that Jesus was really dead, to argue against those
who may have said that all that happened was that Jesus
revived after a long coma, and it is possible that this polemic
note was the reason for the presence of this phrase from the
first. But it could also have been that the early Jerusalem
church had already developed an interest in the place of Jesus'
tomb itself and hence the reference to burial. Perhaps the most
likely explanation is that it provides additional strengthening
to the previous clause 'he died for our sins' in the same way
that 'he appeared to Cephas and the Twelve' strengthens 'he
was raised to life on the third day'. Peter and the Twelve
belong very much to the Jerusalem tradition in its earliest
years. Remember that this is before Luke; there is nothing

here to suggest that the creed refers just to a few weeks after Passover; the appearances listed could span a year or more (the Twelve indicates the corporate body at Jerusalem and we do not have to think in Luke's terms about there being only eleven of them, since Judas had hanged himself and Matthias had not yet been chosen to fill the vacancy). The five hundred brethren are not elsewhere mentioned; James becomes the leader of the Jerusalem church after some years, and the phrase 'all the apostles' is clearly wider than the Twelve and may reflect the later tradition of using this word for the specially authorized disciples and their helpers. By including the appearance to himself, and it is almost universally assumed that Paul is referring to the experience on the Damascus road, about a year after the crucifixion, Paul indicates clearly that the Lukan timetable is no part of his tradition. Because of his insistence that the appearance to him is of the same order as the appearance to Peter and the others, no 'ascension' intervenes to alter the character of what is seen; if his was a vision so was theirs, if his was the sight of an actual body so was theirs. It also shows that Paul's concern at this point is not proving the resurrection of Christ but the authentication of his own gospel. To have seen Jesus is to be an authorized preacher of his gospel, an apostle. Paul is claiming that the gospel that he has preached is the same as the other apostles preach and that he and they share the same commissioning – they have been sent by the risen Christ. We learn a little more about how the earliest church saw the rising itself from the second of Paul's quoted credal fragments.

Romans 1.3 speaks of God's Son 'born of the seed of David according to the flesh but according to the Spirit declared Son of God in power in that he rose from the dead'. This two-fold flesh/spirit division is characteristic of Greek thinking, and of Paul himself, but other features of this fragment, the resurrection's being the declaration by God that Jesus is Son of God are not typical of Paul who tends to talk of Jesus always having been God's Son. Here the resurrection is God's vindication of Jesus, His 'yes' to all that Jesus said and did, and thus a real change in the status of Jesus, and in his ability to effect the salvation of the believer.

The point about the resurrection's being a dramatic change in the status of Jesus is made more forcibly in the third passage where Paul reflects ancient language, *Phil 2.6–11*; after speaking of the Son's voluntary abasement even to death on the cross, he continues, 'wherefore God raised him to the heights and bestowed on him the name above all names.' There is no mention of resurrection here at all; exaltation is another way of talking about the Easter event; and the compartmentalizing, systematizing and timetabling that has subsequently taken place in order to make these various ideas more reconcilable must not hide from us the variety of images or the true unity. The raising to life again is at one and the same time also the vindication, coronation and exaltation to power; some early Christians preferred one way of speaking and some another. The Epistle to the Hebrews for example and the Gospel of St John tend to proclaim the meaning of Jesus predominantly in terms of exaltation, entering heaven and going to the Father, with only occasional use of the idea of raising from the dead, but this does not mean that neither Hebrews nor John makes what Resurrection is confessing central to their Gospel.

Other, and possibly still earlier, ways of proclaiming the significance of Easter can be found in the Books of Acts; written a decade or more after the Pauline letters, it does seem as if the historian Luke was using some very early material when he composes the speeches of the first apostles. Particularly interesting is *Acts 3.12–26* where Jesus is presented as the servant and Mosaic prophet sent to Israel whom, as usual, the Jewish people had rejected, persecuted and killed even though they did it in ignorance: '*God however raised him from the dead, and to that fact we are the witnesses; and it is the name of Jesus, through the faith in it*' that has caused the miracle of the healing of the man by the Beautiful Gate. Peter continues, and we should mark this, for perhaps this is the earliest version of the Easter Gospel, and one that ties in most closely with what Jesus himself preached before it happened.

Now you must repent and turn to God, so that your sins

> *may be wiped out, and so that the Lord may send the time of comfort. Then he will send you the Christ he has predestined, that is Jesus, whom heaven must keep till the universal restoration comes which God proclaimed . . . You are the heirs of the prophets, the heirs of the covenant God made with our ancestors when he told Abraham 'in your offspring all the families of the earth will be blessed'; It was for you in the first place that God raised up his servant and sent him to bless you by turning every one of you from your wicked ways'.*

Resurrection here is not the eschatological event, which is still in the future, waiting for the faith of the people which contributes to the possibility of it happening; resurrection is rather the vindication of Jesus as the true prophet and Messiah. Luke's own theology of resurrection is a good deal more than this, as his Gospel and the rest of Acts show, but here we may well be in touch with the earliest understanding of it.[39] The part played by the faith of Christians, both in the healing of the man, and in bringing about the coming of Christ, is notable.

In *Acts 2.24–36* we hear the resurrection proclaimed as 'according to the Scriptures'; Jesus is shown to have fulfilled three prophecies 1) he did not remain in Hades 2) his body did not experience corruption; and 3) he was exalted to the right hand of God. How much the details of Scriptural passages actually shaped the resurrection traditions, as they certainly seem to have done the passion narratives we can only guess at, but it may be that Luke's own insistence that the Jesus the disciples saw during the 40 days was clearly physical, had something to do with this passage from Psalm 16.

The Lord: Risen, Ascended, Glorified

When the early Christians proclaimed that 'Jesus is risen' they professed

> their allegiance: 1) to God, as being He who raised Jesus from the dead, and accordingly, 2) to Jesus, as the 'Lord'

whom God appointed through the resurrection: 'If on
your lips is the confession, "Jesus is Lord" and in your
heart the faith that God raised him from the dead then
you will find salvation' (*Romans 10.9*). The resurrection
of Jesus was not preached as an event which only
affected Jesus himself, but as an event concerning also
the relationship between God and men at the end of
time, concerning man's eternal salvation or damnation.
Through his resurrection Jesus was appointed to an
official position, to that of Saviour of those who belong
to God. Since the resurrection, God has transferred to
the risen Jesus the operation of his redeeming act at the
Day of Salvation, as he promised those who are faithful
to him; and Jesus, since the resurrection, is for God's
faithful what God himself is to his people, namely 'the
Lord'.[40]

Nothing that any subsequent New Testament writer put
into words about how the first disciples came to believe that
Jesus was risen, or how they received their commission to
preach Christ as Lord, and we are going on now to consider
Paul and the Gospel writers as they do just that, takes away
from the abiding fact that to believe that Christ is risen is
primarily something about the present and only secondarily a
statement about past history. It is a statement about the
present in terms of one's loyalty, one's conviction about those
human words and actions upon which God Himself has set
His seal and so a statement about one's own present, about
one's values and expectations now. *That* is why the resurrection of Christ is central to the Christian faith, but it is more
the whole Easter event that is central, not so much the word
resurrection. The danger of the speculations about the nature
of Christ's risen body, either between Easter Day and
Ascension or post Ascension, and if there is any difference
between those two, is that these speculations, for that is what
they are, can divert attention into side issues. The historical
dimension of resurrection language must be complimented
and accompanied by the symbolic dimension of ascension

language; to talk too much of Easter and not to link it with Ascension, as Leon-Dufour puts it in a fine passage:[41]

> ultimately reduces the mystery to the level of an unusual and prodigious event. The life of glory then becomes that of Lazarus with something extra. Where has the mystery gone?

That is exactly the point of course that the Bishop of Durham was making when he protested that over-much concentration on the physical nature of the body tended to make people draw the wrong conclusion that the Resurrection was 'a conjuring trick with bones'. There may have been some people who genuinely thought that that phrase was what Dr Jenkins thought the Easter event was, though I doubt it; many more I suspect thought it was a good phrase to use to suggest to people that that was what he thought. In fact, of course, even that aspect of what the disciples experienced is taken perfectly seriously by Dr Jenkins. In the famous *Credo* interview he said that

> there were a series of experiences which convinced, gradually convinced, a growing number of the people who became apostles that Jesus had certainly been dead, certainly buried, and that he wasn't finished but what is more . . . he was raised up, that is to say, the very life and power and purpose and personality which was in him was actually continuing, and was continuing both in the sphere of God and in the sphere of history, so that he was a risen and living presence and possibility

and he rejects in the next reply the likelihood that this was only a subjective experience, believing that God was involved in producing this event for that is the way that God does communicate with people, putting himself into personal and internal events so that there is more that causes it than just our imagination.[42] But I am anticipating now some of the issues that we must turn to when we have looked at some of the next generation of resurrection affirmations which the

New Testament offers us, that is those that come from Paul and the evangelists themselves. To these we now turn.

The Five Main New Testament Witnesses

'Did I not see Jesus our Lord?' asks Paul accusingly when his apostleship is in question. This claim to have been chosen by the risen Jesus to have a manifestation of himself and to receive a commission to preach to the Gentiles, must not be thought of solely as a vision, or even something seen with the eyes, although that was obviously a part of it. In *Phil. 3.10* he calls it 'knowing Christ as Lord' or 'gaining him' or 'being incorporate with him' and in *Gal.1.16* God 'chose to reveal his Son to me and through me'. It was a total experience of being captured, claimed, enlightened, illuminated by the one he had fought against and resisted as an enemy of the Law, now shown to him as vindicated by God and declared to be the true means of salvation. So the impetuous, vigorous and expansive Saul transfers to Jesus all the zeal and devotion that he had previously shown to the Law; only now he saw the Law as something that had been outside himself, tyrannizing over him and preventing him from doing the very things that mattered most whereas he saw Jesus as someone in whom he was incorporated so that he was part of Jesus and Jesus was the whole of him. Moreover it was not merely an individual matter, for the body of Jesus of which he had now become a member was his fellow Christians so he was part of them and they were part of him 'in Christ'. The body of Christ is an absolutely central concept here for Paul, because it was not only what he had seen alive but it was what he had been persecuting.[43] Christians were not just believers in Jesus, they were part of him, his very body and blood; they were actual sharers now in the very life of the risen and ascended Son; they shared the first fruits of this physically in their communal meal and morally in the virtues and graces which the Holy Spirit was gently propelling them into; and these first fruits gave them the assurance that they were destined to share more fully in it in the life to come. This is why the resurrection of dead Christians is integrally tied up with the resurrection of Jesus and why Paul argues in *1 Cor. 15.12–19* that to deny one is actually to deny the other.

In *1 Cor. 15.35* he deals with a question that the Corinthians have asked which is substantially the same as Baruch's 'How are the dead raised? In what kind of body?' and the answer that Paul gives is of great interest. (Paul believed that the body of the risen Christ was the very thing that constituted the life of believers, therefore what he says about the nature of the believers' bodies after death and in the risen life must be what he would say, were he asked, about the nature of Jesus' risen body.) It is very possible that Paul does not give the same answer as some other first century Christians – including other writers of the New Testament – would have done, but his own view is stated forcefully enough: 'Someone may ask "How are dead people raised, and what sort of body do they have when they come back"' (the similarity with Baruch is startling – but the answer is very different):

> They are stupid questions; whatever you sow in the ground has to die before it is given new life, and the thing that you sow is not what is going to come; you sow a bare grain, say of wheat or something like that, and then God gives it the sort of body that he has chosen: each sort of seed gets its own sort of body . . . It is the same with the resurrection of the dead; the thing that is sown is perishable but what is raised is imperishable; the thing that is sown is contemptible but what is raised is glorious; the thing that is sown is weak but what is raised is powerful; when it is sown it embodies the soul (or, is a natural body); when it is raised it embodies the spirit (or, is a spiritual body) . . . The first man being from the earth is earthly by nature; the second man is from heaven; as this earthly man was, so are we on earth; and as the heavenly man is, so are we in heaven . . . Or else brothers, put it this

way; flesh and blood cannot inherit the kingdom of
God.

The analogy with seed sown in the ground is crucial; it is the
same seed, that is the personal identity that so many modern
interpreters seem to see as the importance of the physical
resurrection; but with Paul the whole point is that it is not
physical – all that dies in the earth for it cannot inherit the
kingdom of God – it is something totally transformed,
looking different, more glorious, more powerful and
imperishable that is raised. It is useful to remember this image
of Paul's when we turn, as we do now, to the narratives in the
four gospels, because several of them suggest that the disciples
did not immediately recognize that the one they saw was Jesus
– the Emmaus disciples are the best examples of this, as they
walked with him and heard him expound the Scriptures for a
substantial amount of time before they recognized him only in
the breaking of bread in the house; but Mary in the garden
and the disciples fishing on the lake also seemed to need a
special word or gesture before they knew who he was.

The four gospel accounts are different; they agree on some
elements, they disagree on others. For those who like to read
them as different eye-witness accounts of the same series of
events, there is the challenge of trying to conflate them so they
do give different episodes of the same series. We all know the
story of Frank Morrison, who wrote 'Who Moved the Stone?'
who set out to prove that the accounts were not reconcilable
and was persuaded by the evidence that they were, and so
wrote a very different book from the one he had intended.
No-one denies that the conflation exercise can be done if you
try hard enough, although the major discrepancy – whether
the disciples went back immediately to Galilee or stayed a
week or more in Jerusalem, takes a lot of ingenuity to
reconcile. But most Gospel commentators do not attempt
such an exercise because they do not think that the Gospels
are trying to do that job at all; they are not piecing together
historical evidence, but using the historical traditions that
they have to hand to assure their hearers of the truth that they

are proclaiming now; they are not trying to solve a detective's jigsaw but preaching the presence of Jesus alive among their readers and hearers.

Mark is probably the earliest of the four (c. 60 AD). His narrative is the most intriguing of all, and if it was meant to end where the original text now breaks off (*16:8*) the sense of mystery is heightened almost to breaking point. Mary Magdalene and her companion come to the tomb, the burial having been mentioned in the previous verses; but then the heavenly action comes crashing in, the stone is rolled away, the heavenly being tells them they are looking in the wrong place if they want Jesus, 'he is risen, he is not here'. They must go to Galilee if they want to see him; but, confronted with this act of God the disciples, as so often in Mark, are uncomprehending, terror-struck and even disobedient, 'they said nothing to anyone, for they were afraid'. Some scholars of course argue that the original Mark must have gone on to narrate appearances in Galilee, but as it stands, ignoring the later endings, Mark has no appearances, no faithful disciples, just a stupendous act of God, confronted with which the search for the body becomes pointless: 'he is not here. Go.' Mark we say is the earliest of the four gospels, but even that is not very early; it is almost certainly later than Paul and both of these must have been preceded by fifteen-twenty years preaching and teaching of the gospel. In trying to penetrate back into this period, most scholars will affirm that in Mark we have the indications of two of the very earliest traditions: 1) that the first hints that the disciples were experiencing a changed attitude to their crucified master came from the women, Mary Magdelene in particular, and 2) that it was in Galilee that groups of disciples saw the Lord and began to preach that he was risen. However, before long those who had seen the risen Jesus were regarded in a very specific way by the rest of the believers in the early church: these people were seen as not just those who in fact had started the preaching of the gospel, but as those who must have been *authorized* to do so. They were the commissioned apostles, *sent* by the risen Lord. This attitude meant that the women's witness tended to become minimized or even ignored, since the social situation of the first century world, particularly in Judaism, did not encourage a public lead to be taken in preaching by women. So the emphasis begins to be put on the appearances to Church leaders, and of course anyone claiming to have the authority to preach would need to be one who had 'seen the Lord'. Paul's tradition in *1 Cor. 15* already shows this tendency with Peter coming first in the list, and James also being mentioned. Mark shows the beginning of this process of the diminishing of the women with his emphasis on their silence, and the hint that Peter and the disciples will see Jesus in Galilee.

Matthew takes this development further. We have now appearances in Galilee where Jesus comes to see his apostles and give them what is without doubt a commissioning charge. The implication in Matthew is that the disciples go to Galilee in obedience to a command from Jesus that that is where he would meet them, but there is a fair amount of scepticism about as to whether that is the reason, and a feeling that more likely they had fled back to Galilee in despair after the apparent execution of their leader and failure of their movement (as John 21 implies). The whole scene is meant to recall Moses on Mount Sinai as the new Moses commissions his new prophets and servants. The great contribution of Matthew to the resurrection traditions is this clear link with authority not only to preach but also to baptize and the association of both activities with the tremendous consequence of the Easter event, the actual meaning of resurrection, 'I am with you, even to the end of time'. Matthew also adds a few other little elements that most commentators say reflect the preaching needs of the church situation for which Matthew is writing. He develops the sense of expectation even more than Mark by concentrating on the tomb and the guard placed upon it. He heightens the mystery of the angel at the tomb by asserting that there was a thunderstorm, and that the angel came and sat on the stone, to the terror of the guards. Is this elaboration what normally happens in the process of story-telling – we all do it, in the innocent pursuit of making the narrative effective – or is it additional bits of historical memory? Matthew counteracts what is probably a Jewish reaction to the preaching of the resurrection, the insinuation that all that happened was that the disciples had come and stolen the body, by the story of the bribing of the guards. Again, though it could by chance be another bit of actual memory, it is more generally taken as ammunition for Matthew's church in its conflict with Jewish detractors – when you are sure of the heart of the matter, details like these are almost debating points.

Luke gives us the Markan narrative in outline, but follows it up with two new elements – the walk to Emmaus and an appearance of Jesus to the Eleven at Jerusalem, which is clearly the climax of the one day into which Luke puts all his Easter events. Later, at the beginning of Acts, he extends the period by the symbolic 40 days, but in the Gospel not only all the appearances but also the visible ascension occur on the one day. But the chronology of it is not important to Luke as chronology – Luke is not asserting that that is how it happened, he is not that kind of historian. He is working to a magnificent scheme which is meant to show his readers that they are part of a great movement of history from Jerusalem – where the death and resurrection of Jesus took place – out to all corners of the world. Luke announces at the beginning of his Gospel that his purpose is to put things 'in order' (*Luke 1.3*) so he arranges the climax to be, like Matthew, an appearance of the Lord to his disciples to commission them for their work. Only, unlike Matthew, it takes place in Jerusalem, not Galilee; and on the first day not weeks later; and Luke ends with Jesus departing from them into heaven instead declaring his presence with them for ever.

Luke's 40 day period with the Ascension concluding it is introduced, I think, for two reasons: 1) he wants his readers to see that the Age of the Incarnation is over; they must not think that the resurrection means the prolongation of Jesus' presence with us. It is important for Luke that Jesus has gone; and although he will come again at the End, we are now in the Age of the Holy Spirit. That is the manner of God's presence with us now, through the Spirit of Jesus, working in new ways and giving Christians the strength for their new tasks. 2) The other reason for introducing the 40 day/Ascension theme is that Luke (and John too) are working among Greek-thinking people. For them it would be easy to think of Jesus as a disembodied spirit and thus nothing new – for the pagan world was supposed to be full of such ghosts – so they would have fitted Jesus as one more spirit into their old well-known, natural order of things. So both Luke and John emphasize Jesus' physical identity with Jesus of Nazareth: 'touch me and see', 'reach here your hands', 'he ate before their eyes' *etc*. Both also recognize that some of Jesus' appearances were not physical or material in character – Jesus vanishes, he passes through locked doors – so there is a variety here which we must recognize. But if, like Luke and John, you have committed yourself to some element of physical presence you have spatial questions on your hands, where was he in the meantime? where is he now? will he appear to us as he did then? Removal into a spatial heaven is the only solution to show that whatever happened during that period it is not to be expected now. I am not saying that Luke invented the Ascension event to get out of this difficulty. To people who thought like that, perhaps it had to happen like that. The same applies to the empty tomb traditions; they are not of the essence of the resurrection, even though they belong among its early strata; why are they not 'of the essence'; because if Jesus' body is the same body as that he had on earth but totally transformed, as a plant which comes from a seed, and if we are to share in the same resurrected life even though our bodies decompose and are burnt in the incinerator then Jesus' risen body is a reality wherever and whatever happened to the actual flesh, bones and sinews. Of course, if like most first century Jews you could not see that, and could only believe that it was Jesus if it was the physical presence that they saw, then perhaps God could have arranged it that that was what they saw; there could have been an empty tomb for them, if that is how they could believe. It is not necessary for us, but perhaps it was for them.

John's two final chapters make it very difficult for anyone who wants to harmonize the accounts. John, as much as the other evangelists, is writing in order to help us believe not to inform us about history. The Thomas episode takes up the theme of the doubt of the apostles, which we have heard about in Matthew and Luke; its purpose is not to argue for the physical reality of the body – that is a side issue – but to lead up to the Lord's statement directly for us: 'Happy are those who have never seen me and yet have found faith' (20.29); this of course is the climax of the whole gospel and fits with John's insistence all along that faith is a spiritual truth not the same as persuasion through proof which is a normal process of human reasoning. Earlier in the chapter John has signified that Ascension and Pentecost have already happened by the evening of the first Easter day; ascension because while Mary is forbidden to touch him because he has 'not yet' ascended, Thomas is invited to touch that evening and the Spirit is breathed on them, which John has already declared (in 16.7) cannot happen until Jesus has gone to his Father.

The added chapter 21 builds on the traditions that some of the disciples went back to Galilee and came to believe in Jesus there; it then develops into passages about Peter and John and their own special relationship to the Lord. But I think that John does make us reflect that the experiences that caused the first disciples to start preaching that a crucified prophet was the lord of the world and saviour of mankind must have been of a very varied kind, and have lasted over quite a long period. One thing they all required however was the venture of faith.

The Resurrection and Faith

The moment we start thinking that anything *proves* the resurrection, whether it is the empty tomb, or the wounds in the side of the risen body or the compared testimonies of the New Testament writers, then I am sure we begin to go wrong. This is why I feel in my bones that those who say that their faith in the risen Lord is being undermined by those who publicly state their doubts about the physical nature of Christ's risen body are speaking actually from a position of unfaith; they are not simple believers who must be humoured lest they get upset: on the contrary, they must not be conceded to for to give way to them is to give way on the very nature of faith itself. I quote from Willi Marxsen:[44]

> If we insist that the events must be viewed in 'physical' terms if we are able to believe, if we insist that faith must be faith in the reliability of the witnesses and that the legitimation of Jesus must be thus secured before we can commit ourselves to him, if we say that true faith is impossible without this legitimation, then we are rejecting faith as a challenge, as a venture. And that means we are refusing to believe ... A verifiable resurrection, with its multiplicity of proofs would have altered everything in one respect. Jesus would have received his legitimation. Who he was would now be a matter of certainty. The demand for signs would, so to speak, have been fulfilled. It would no longer have been a venture to enter the life of faith; indeed it would have been a counsel of wisdom.

The faith that is at the heart of Christianity is the faith that affirms that the way of Jesus is the way to be followed whether or not we see the outcome or see why it is right. Nothing must be placed as a barrier to seeing that. One way of affirming this commitment is to say 'Jesus is risen'; that is ancient and respectable language; it derives from the language that the earliest Christians used to affirm the faith. But it is the faith that matters, not the language. The real heresy is not to make Jesus' cause the cause for which we live. We are all so busy avoiding the real challenge that controversy is a nice diversion. The great task of theology, ancient or modern, is to let the very essence of God's mysterious truth and all its implications for human behaviour stand out clearly before men and women so that they can be confronted by the challenge itself and not be diverted from this challenge or prevented from seeing the truth by considerations that are ultimately only of secondary importance. The study of antiquity is an essential component part of theology but over-much concentration on what happened in the past, what the resurrection involved then, can hide the actual challenge of the resurrection from modern believers. Similarly, speculative philosophy and the strenuous use of reason is also an essential component part of theology but over-much concentration on what our contemporary culture will permit us to contemplate or on what we conceive to be possible can hide from us the uniqueness and mysteriousness of what God may have done only once in history.[44] So the study of antiquity and the speculative use of reason are parts of theology but not its heart; its very central task is uncovering afresh for each generation the truth as God has made it known. When it does that, theology is both the queen of sciences and the servant of the Church.

PART 2

Whom Do We Believe?

4

Jesus: Man?

Introduction

What is 'Christology' and why is it worth so much of the thinking energy of earnest Christians over the centuries? The answer to the first question is easy. Christology is a conveniently short technical word for the language that has grown up in the Christian tradition about Jesus, the language that tries to explain why Jesus is important and what part he plays in the purposes of God and in the history of mankind. The second question is about Christianity as a whole; if Christianity is worth anyone's time then understanding about Christ is too, for Christianity is about Jesus if it is about anything. 'Whom say you that I am?' is the most penetrating question that Jesus addresses to any generation.

So the traditional language must be studied. 'New Testament Christology' is about the various ways in which New Testament writers tried to do justice to Jesus of Nazareth and to write something that helped their early Christian readers to see why the coming of Jesus meant that everyone, Jews and Gentiles, now had to think of God – and respond to Him – in a new way. The New Testament writers had to find words and phrases that were appropriate to Jesus as He is both *before* and *after* crucifixion; they found words like 'messiah', 'lord', 'prophet, priest and king', 'Way, Truth and Life', and phrases like 'born of a woman, born under the law', 'image of the invisible god' and 'he sits at the right hand of God'. Some of them, especially Paul and the authors of the Fourth Gospel and the Letter to the Hebrews, tried to dig deeper than these words and phrases and present something more fully worked out.

51

Traditional, or orthodox Christology refers to the debates that were held in the fourth and fifth centuries AD between Christians who had somewhat differing views about how to define the humanity and divinity of Christ; it refers in particular to the compromise solution that was reached at the Council of Chalcedon in 451 AD; the formula then established, framed in the language of Greek metaphysics, has served the Church pretty well until recent times. In its shortest possible form this definition states that Christ was a single person or entity (*hypostasis*) but composed of two complete and perfect natures (*physis*) one divine, consubstantial with God and the other human, consubstantial with us.

Contemporary Christology means the debates that have taken place in the nineteenth and twentieth centuries, particularly in the last thirty years or so, when this old definition has been put under some considerable strain as a result of the advances in the sum total of human knowledge and the new attitudes to historical evidence that are characteristic of our times in every field of study. The bibliography in English alone on this one aspect of theology is probably as large as any other. (A select list is provided below[1])

We have only been reflecting a world-wide interest in Christology however and many of the books that are important were written on the continent or in America. Let us dig down deeper then into what has been concerning our Christian thinkers for so long.

If 'Theology' is taking rational trouble about the ultimate mystery underlying the universe, then 'Christology' is taking rational trouble about the way in which this mystery has expressed itself over the centuries in the processes of nature and history coming to fulfilment in mankind and in one man in particular. For when the Jews talked about the Anointed One (in their Hebrew language 'messiah' and in Greek – in which the New Testament was written – 'Christos') they meant the one who was effecting God's purposes in the world, thus maintaining that the clue to the universe is to be found in persons and their concerns. In other words, Christology is about the very centre of Christianity, and is that which we

Christians claim to have learnt about God and ourselves because of Jesus Christ.

But it is not only important; it is exciting. I think this is the area of theology where not only has most attention been recently given but also the area where the most arresting and hopeful things have been said. So often even positive criticism of established positions and doctrines sounds destructive and negative in the ears of the faithful who only hear about it at second hand; but one only has to read a little among all the words of recent Christology to see that everyone who has written, whether radical or conservative, has a deep devotion to Christ and an enthusiasm to explore, strengthen and extend his influence in the world and the significance of His life and death. You can also pick up some new lines of thought that stretch your imagination into new glimpses of *why* Jesus Christ is the one most important fact in the world; those who have dipped into the heady world of Teilhard de Chardin's *Le Milieu Divin* or David Jenkins' *The Glory of Man* will know what I mean. To study this subject is not only important therefore; it also shows that the great weight of thought and prayer which the church has devoted to this subject in this century has deepened and widened our understanding and commitment to Christ, not otherwise.

Is Jesus A Man? and Is Jesus God?

These questions are both questions which orthodox Christology answers with a 'No'; a qualified 'No' certainly but nevertheless No: Orthodox Christology, insofar as it is defined by the Council of Chalcedon, has to say that Jesus Christ was a divine person who took human nature to Himself but could not be a human person; so Jesus was *man* but not *a man*; that is what orthodox Christology has to say about the first question. The 'No' to the second question presupposes that the word 'God' here is a noun; Jesus is not all there is of God, he is not God pure and simple; but of course orthodox Christology would answer 'Yes' if the question was 'Is Jesus divine?' for it teaches that he is the image of God, the Word of God, the Son of God, he is the second person of the Trinity which is God, yes; he is true God from true God, yes; he is God if the word is an adjective; but not God, full stop. We are here taken straight away into the heart of the problem of Christology, ancient and modern. But not all Christology has to be in terms of humanity and divinity; classical Reformed Christology makes great use of the three Biblical titles of 'Prophet, Priest and King' and the Fourth Gospel asserts that the Risen Christ is 'the Way, the Truth and the Life'. I doubt whether any Christian would deny that *in some senses* Jesus is these things but there would have to be discussion about whether it was helpful to say Jesus is priest or king and whether He was or is *the* Way, Truth and Life and what it would mean if you said He was. So as assertions even these are not immune from probing. They have, of course, indisputable Biblical pedigrees and have a distinct advantage over any metaphysical or ontological language that, at least for modern minds, they have unmistakable moral and ethical implications; and it must be a prerequisite for any effective Christology that it must not only make great claims for Jesus but should also help speaker and hearer to love, worship and obey him.

A Christological Sketch Map

A look at the early New Testament writings will quickly make it plain that Jesus' disciples knew him to be a man who was not only close to God but also inspired by God and chosen by Him for the immense task of proclaiming and ushering in the Kingdom. At the very least, people used the respectful title 'Sir' – *kurios* translated Lord; others called him Prophet or Teacher (Rabbi); in a great rush of enthusiasm and insight, Peter at Caesarea Philippi calls Him '*Messiah (Christ)* that is, the human being whom God will use at the appointed time to restore the kingdom to Israel and cause her to triumph; the word denotes the king of Israel, the annointed one, and the expected messiah was to be a king even more gloriously than his ancestor David. It seems that Jesus was not too happy about being hailed as Christ; he would rather his disciples saw him as the agent and representative of God in bringing in a rather different kind of kingdom. It is crucial to realize that on Jewish lips *God's Son* did not mean a divine being from heaven, but *a human being adopted and chosen by God for a specially close relationship to Him*; just as there were many sons of God in Israel's history and indeed Israel herself was known as the sons (children) of God; so when the Messiah came he would be son in a very special sense: the son rather than a son of God. So when Matthew adds the phrase 'Son of the living God' to the word 'Messiah' in his version of Peter's confession at Caesarea Philippi he is not saying anything very different from Mark and Luke's versions,[2] and anyone confessing Jesus as Messiah might very well also have claimed that he was not only a son, but also the very special son of God.

After the Resurrection experiences, the first disciples had to say even more startling things about their risen master; they did not need to unsay the things they had said before, simply to add to them. The evidence for what they said at first is mainly in the speeches in the Book of Acts. Here are two examples:

Men of Israel, hear these words; Jesus of Nazareth, a man attested to you by God with mighty works and wonders and signs which God did through him in your midst, as you yourselves know – this Jesus, delivered up according to the definite plan and foreknowledge of God, you crucified and killed by the hands of lawless men. But God raised him up, having loosened the pangs of death, because it was not possible for him to be held by it . . . This Jesus God raised up, and of that we are all witnesses. Being therefore exalted at the right hand of God, and having received from the Father the promise of the Holy Spirit, he has poured out this which you see and hear . . . Let all the house of Israel know assuredly that God has made him both Lord and Christ, this Jesus whom you crucified.[3]

The God of our fathers raised Jesus whom you killed by hanging him on a tree. God exalted him at his right hand as Leader and Saviour, to give repentence to Israel and forgiveness of sins.[4]

Note what is happening in this the first New Testament Christological pattern: their memory of Jesus of Nazareth is denoted by terms like 'a man attested to you by God', 'God's servant', 'a prophet' – what I am going to call *Man language*. Then comes the great event of Good Friday/Easter Day. A contrast is made between the treatment given to Jesus by the Jews and by God. The first Christians' proclamation of what God has exalted Jesus to is in terms like 'Lord and Christ', 'Leader and Saviour' – what I am going to call *God language*. Now it is undisputed that this is the first Christological pattern in the New Testament; we should pay particular attention to it because it is far more important in the New Testament than is commonly recognized. We tend to read Paul, John and the author of Hebrews in the light of the later developments that I am now going on to outline and we are inclined to think too readily that they have 'moved on' to something far more complicated when perhaps what is happening is that all three of them are simply introducing minor modifications into this, the basic New Testament Christology.

God is eternal, that is, beyond time, outside time altogether; but the human mind finds it difficult, if not impossible to imagine this and so thinks of it as everlasting-ness, existing in time for all periods, from the very beginning to the very end; let us recognize now that this is not quite the same thing as eternity and might lead us astray in our thinking. As far as the knowledge of God is concerned it has turned His omniscience – His knowledge of everything to do with the world – into foreknowledge, knowing what He is going to do *before* He does it. Now insofar as the mind of God is conceiving the Saviour who is to come and this conceiving, instead of being thought of as outside time, is thought of as happening in time, the coming Saviour is thought of as already existing during the centuries before the Incarnation. To help this process he becomes identified with those other aspects of God working in the world for man's salvation, the Word of God, the Wisdom of God, the Spirit of God, and, for Jews especially, the Law of God. So the Son, Lord, Saviour that Jesus has become is identified with all the other facets of God and the Son becomes thought of as pre-existent. This led to some confusion of language and gradually Word, and to a less extent Wisdom, become alternative words for the Son. The Spirit however is kept back from total identity with him. (Paul could never make up his mind whether the Spirit was the Spirit of Jesus or of God and this confusion has lasted right through the history of the Church.)

The result of this development was that the Son was now thought of as eternal, pre-existing the birth, baptism or resurrection of Jesus. So now language about 'God sending His Son' which can belong quite happily in the first, basic pattern, becomes 'the Son coming down, taking flesh, or becoming man'; now we have the full Nicene theology of the three eternal persons of the Godhead. Now two completely new Christological problems have arrived on the scene; is Jesus of Nazareth also some kind of divine being and, is the Risen Lord and Christ still a man? The early church also found a third problem, which does not much exercise us now: did Jesus as man therefore have some kind of pre-existence before his birth at Bethlehem? Now it is not part of my present task to argue how much of this later development appears already in the New Testament; I think all students of the Scriptures would agree that some moves in this direction were made by Paul, John and the author of Hebrews but whether any of them actually affirmed the pre-existence of the Son (as distinct from the pre-existence of the Word) is being disputed.[5] What is clear, and this is what concerns us, is that by the fourth century AD all Christian theologians were thinking in a pattern nearer to this second one than to the first.

The third and final pattern that should be considered in this sketchy outline of Christology represents a definite moving away from the fundamental shape of the first pattern. There the resurrection was a crucial and significant point, *the* crucial and significant point, in what God did for Jesus and through Him for the world. But because the Risen Jesus is exactly the same person as the incarnate Jesus and the church was coming to feel that what is said of the Risen Christ must be true also before the crucifixion, and vice versa, there is a distinct lessening of the importance of the Resurrection, and a corresponding heightening in the importance of the Incarnation. I think that this movement is much less apparent in the New Testament itself, although there are a few slight indications of it[6] but all historians would agree that it becomes quite dominant after the New Testament time, and quite soon after it too. This development makes more difficult the solving of the two new Christological problems mentioned above. Everything that is said about Jesus has now got to apply both to Jesus of Nazareth, the incarnate Word who taught his disciples, worked miracles, prayed to His Father and – very difficult for the early fathers – suffered pain and died on the cross, and to the Risen Lord, who reigns triumphant in heaven, whose body is mystically present on earth and who will return at the end of time to claim his kingdom on earth and present it gloriously to the Father.

This then is an outline of what Christology is and I can now turn to look at it further in the light of my question 'Is Jesus a man?'; we must see why the orthodox Christology says 'No' to this and why nearly all contemporary theological writers think that Christology needs to be modified at this point so that it says, 'Yes'.

The Humanity of Jesus

Everyone agrees that the Chalcedonian definition was a compromise; there is nothing wrong with it for being that; very often in intellectual matters as well as practical ones that is the only way forward. It is *a way forward*, and not only a marking of time, because the effort of defining things more closely between two points of view often does contribute a new understanding of that bit of the truth that is in both of them. The compromise was between two ways of dealing with the problems of starting with a divine being. By the fourth and fifth centuries AD the majority of Christians accepted these as the basic presuppositions. In the East, where most of the speculative thinking of Christianity was being done, (the West was more of a practical turn of mind, perhaps because its language was Latin rather than Greek, and even its major thinkers, like Tertullian and Augustine, could be thought of having a practical rather than a speculative bent), the two schools of thought were centred round the two great patriarchates of Alexandria in Egypt and Antioch in Syria. The former tended to start with the assumption that the Word was basically and permanently the second Person of the Trinity and talked of the incarnation primarily in terms of the Word 'taking to himself human flesh, or humanity' while the Antiochene tradition tended to say that the Word 'became man' and functioned entirely and completely as a man as well as being the eternal Word of God.

It is the second of these that we shall be mainly concerned with because the Antiochenes started with the conviction that any account of the way that the Incarnate Word functioned must recognize that he became a man and, *just because he was a man*, was our Saviour. In this they had the support of many passages of Scripture, particularly in the Epistle to the Hebrews; here are two of them:

> Since therefore the children share in flesh and blood, he himself likewise partook of the same nature . . . therefore he had to be made like his brethren in every respect, so that he might become a merciful and faithful high priest in the service of God, to make expiation for the sins of people. For because he himself has suffered and been tempted, he is able to help those who are tempted (*Hebrews* 2.14,17,18).[4]

In the days of his flesh Jesus offered up prayers and

supplications, with loud cries and tears, to him who was able to save him from death, and he was heard for his godly fear. Although he was a Son, he learned obedience through what he suffered; and being made perfect he became the source of eternal salvation to all who obey him (*Hebrews 5.7–9a*).[5]

Their interests were strongly *historical* (the texts of Scripture are to be understood in their plain meaning and not allegorized into some mystical sense, so when the New Testament says that Jesus suffered or did not know something it meant it) and *evangelical* (they were concerned to show how the Incarnation actually saved mankind by taking our manhood and purifying it; what therefore was not assumed was not redeemed they said, so it was crucial that Jesus was in every sense a man in order that men could be saved through him). But the result was that they had to hold a *two-fold or dualist Christology*. Since the Word of God was completely and in every sense divine (*of one ousia-substance-with the Father*) and yet was also a distinct entity of the Godhead, a separate *hypostasis-persona* – not just a mode of its being, and since when this Word came down from heaven he became a real and complete man *of one ousia-substance with us* and a real man with a human soul and spirit *hypostasis-persona*, then you can see why the resulting Christology was two-fold. It was extremely difficult to give any convincing explanation of how such a being was a unity or could function as one person; indeed, in Latin, He was explicitly *two persons*, even though this idea with its consequence of two centres of consciousness was not really intended by those speaking Greek and meaning two hypostases (entities or subjects). They were quite happy, as many Christians have been since, to talk of Jesus at one time functioning as a human being, and being tempted, being angry, suffering pain and not knowing the future and at another time functioning as a divine being, in total control and knowing everything.

But what else could they do? The alternative was to accept the Alexandrian way of thinking, which, to preserve the unity of the Incarnate Word, ran the risk of denying a complete humanity; theirs was a *single or Monist Christology* which started from the presupposition that the divine person of the Word must not be divided so that, however perfect was the humanity assumed by the Word, it must not be a separate hypostasis; after the condemnation of Apollinarius (*c.*310–*c.*390) who said that the Word assumed only human flesh, not a human soul, the Alexandrians had to maintain a complete humanity but it was assumed, some would say subsumed, into the person of the divine Word, so that the Incarnate One was unquestionably one. If the danger of the Antiochene approach was that they could not give a convincing explanation of the one Christ, the danger of the Alexandrian was that they could not give a convincing explanation of the man Jesus.

The crucial phrases of the compromise effected by the Council of Chalcedon (AD 451) are:

> Our Lord Jesus Christ is one and the same Son, the same perfect in Godhead and the same perfect in manhood, truly God and truly man, the same of a rational soul and body, consubstantial with the Father in Godhead, and the same consubstantial with us in manhood, like us in all things except sin . . . made known in two natures, the difference of the natures being by no means removed because of the union, but the property of each nature being preserved and coalescing in one prosopon and one hypostasis, not parted or divided into two prosopa, but one and the same Son.

This is unquestionably a magnificent statement, a fine compromise; its intention to do justice to all that was most dear to Christians of that time is apparent at once; the best testimony it could receive is that it has received the general assent of the majority of Christians ever since, and stands as the classic statement of Christian doctrine on the subject. Nevertheless, even in its own day, it was achieved at a price; it forced the Nestorian and Monophysite churches out of communion with the Catholic church to this day and, many would argue, has forced upon the Eastern and Western

Catholic churches so strong a version of the Johannine Christ that the Christ of the synoptic Gospels and of Hebrews has been interpreted away. The compromise was effected by means of the doctrine of the *hypostatic union*; this is the assumption that the human nature did not have an hypostasis of its own but found its expression in the eternal hypostasis of the Word – the human nature was 'anhypostatic'. Now if I use the Latin word instead of the Greek word of the actual definition, you will see the difficulty; the theory is that the human nature did not have a person of its own but found its expression in the eternal person of the Word – the human nature was 'impersonal' – to put it very simply, the human nature had not got any human person to express itself through; the qualities of humanity were there without a human being. We must not, of course, import into this word any of the more recent implications of 'impersonal' like indifferent, callous or lacking personality; it is after all a translation of a purely ontological term 'hypostasis'. But it did give, and does give, ancient and modern Antiochenes many qualms about how seriously the real humanity of Jesus is being taken. An example of the language that was not infrequently used was that, since Jesus himself was divine it was only his human flesh not his divine self that suffered and was tempted; *he* was always in control, always supreme. He may have had human experiences, but he never experienced them as a human. The more extreme examples of this language give the impression of a god play-acting at being human.

The disadvantages of the 'impersonal' (or more accurately 'anhypostatic') humanity of Jesus were realized by orthodox theologians in the decades following Chalcedon. The solution of one of them, Leontius of Byzantium (6th century AD), has been much studied in the twentieth century; this was that Christ's human nature was not without an hypostasis but that the human hypostasis was taken up by and fulfilled in the divine one. How different this really is from Chalcedon is not clear, but it is an attempt to get over the great disadvantage of

all the Greek metaphysical thinking of the patristic period: the
conviction that there must be a fundamental difference
between divinity and humanity, between God and man.
Leonitius' theory of 'enhypostasia' – that the human nature
was not without a hypostasis but had it included within the
divine hypostasis – at least suggests that a real perfect human
being, as an image of God, could find full expression for every
aspect of his character within the individuality of God
Himself. But this particular theory was not taken much note
of, apart from some early Reformed theogians.[8] until the
present century.

Every field of human understanding has been affected by
the huge increase of knowledge in the nineteenth and
twentieth centuries; the application of proper historical
canons of criticism to the Scriptures and to the history of
dogma, for example, means that we no longer see them as a
fixed and uniform, divinely authorized system, eternally valid
and immune from any change. We can now accept and
recognize the variety of ideas in the New Testament and in
history without feeling we must reduce them all to a
conforming system; we can thus listen more seriously to the
actual voices from the past speaking in their own terms. We
do not think that either St John's Gospel or the Chalcedonian
definition have dropped down from heaven and we can look
more critically, and in the end more appreciatively, at both. In
addition, the new insights into the make-up of human
personality and consciousness, into the relation between
individuality and heredity, into a way a person is not static
but shaped by his environment, make it impossible to hold
some of the ancient ontological ideas about natures and
persons, and how they can be independent of each other,
useful as they were in the light of the science of their times. It
is for reasons like this that the vast majority of twentieth
century theologians feel we must, in all our thinking about
Jesus, start with him as a man; he was that if he was anything.
We will want to say more than that about him, a lot more
than that if we are to do justice to the Christian experience of
him over the centuries, but that we must say; and nothing that

we go on to say must undo that first fundamental assertion: Jesus was a man.

Jesus of Nazareth, if this is right, had a human body, mind, will and soul; he had needs, desires and emotions; he must have been conscious of his sexuality and of his ignorance; he must have known fear, love, doubt and anger; his faith, though probably much greater than ours, must have been of the same kind in that it was a venturing out into the unknown, taking a risk, daring to trust that God wanted him to do something whose outcome was uncertain; not a certainty that God would see him through because he knew that he was God but a faith that was prepared to risk all for God's sake. If he was sinless as Hebrews says, it was because of his own will and purity facing the issues and making the right decisions, not because he was God all the time and therefore it was easy; a sinlessness because he could have sinned and did not, not because it was not possible for him to sin, as some quite orthodox theologians have argued in the past. (To put the point simply from children's hymns: it is not so much 'the little Lord Jesus no crying he makes' – not an idea calculated to endear him to any children surely! – but 'tears and smiles like us he knew'.)

Now much has been written very elegantly and excitingly in the last hundred years on this theme and almost all major theologians from Barth and Tillich in the earlier part of the century to contemporary writers make the same point. The heart of the matter can be put thus: the revelation of God that we confess in Jesus, both as truth to know and as act that effects our salvation, is special just because he was a human being and everything he did and said was done and said as one of us; and it is in these very things that we perceive the hand of God and find a new revelation of Him. The God-language, that all Christians find they must use about Jesus if they are to be true to two thousand years of Christian experience, is not lessened by this approach but enhanced and made more believable. The God-language is a declaration of the signifi-cance of this man, linking him to the very purpose and reason of the universe and asserting his relevance to each one of us.

Jesus as Son or Word of God is the subject of the next chapter, but this one cannot end without suggesting that as 'the man for others', and the man who reveals the perfect pattern of human activity – that for which God created us and which we can recover in Christ – and as the pioneer and perfecter of faith, and the man who died for God's cause and because of human sin, we have not neglected the divinity of Jesus but rescued it from superstition and reluctant belief and vindicated it for men and women of the twentieth century.

5

Jesus: God?

Introduction

Some Christians are perhaps surprised to learn that this
question in its simple form must be answered 'No' by
Christian Orthodoxy. *The denial that Jesus is God* pure and
simple is an essential and permanent part of all Christian
thinking, conservative and radical, ancient and modern,
despite what popular piety has sometimes been allowed to
affirm. The fine, but crucial, distinctions between saying that
Jesus is God, which Christian orthodoxy will not allow, and
saying that Jesus is the Son of God, the image of God, the
second Person of the Trinity, God for us, which it will allow,
have not seemed very obvious or important to the ordinary,
worshipping Christian and he has been allowed, and sometimes encouraged, to ignore these distinctions completely. But
on them the whole structure of Christian theology is built:
*theo*logy in the sense of the Christian doctrine of God, and
*Christ*ology in the sense of the Christian doctrine about the
way God has involved Himself in the world in and through
Jesus, depend upon these distinctions from start to finish.
Indeed any Christian, however little he has thought about his
faith in the past, will find himself using distinctions like these
the moment he is involved in explaining or justifying
Christianity to any adherent of a strongly monotheistic faith
like Judaism or Islam and answering questions like 'You say
that you believe in one God like we do – but what about
Jesus, is not he a second god?' or 'is your God called Jesus?' It
is these distinctions, then, in New Testament, traditional and
contemporary language, that we must look at now.

But, at the outset, something should be said about why it is absolutely necessary that some form of God-language is used about Jesus; however impressive and attractive Jesus is in his human nature and person, that is not enough. There have been other human beings in the world who have showed the highest possible virtues; there have been other prophets and revealers of God among whom Moses and Jeremiah to say nothing of Mohammed and Gandhi come readily to mind. Furthermore it has to be pointed out to those who build everything on the attractiveness of Jesus' human character as 'the man for others', and on the power of his devotion and faith, that perhaps too great a reconstruction is being built on too little evidence; the New Testament is first hand evidence of what the earliest Christians believed about Jesus but it does not give us that much absolutely reliable material for building all our assertions about Jesus upon him as man, still less on him as a man. The New Testament writers do not seem to have been so interested in the quality of Jesus' humanity as we must be in the twentieth century and we must beware of reading too much of what we want to find into what they wrote. Something more than the quality of Jesus' humanity is needed to account for the rise and survival of Christianity and I think the heart of it is not that Jesus is God, but that in Jesus God was at work; God, was involved in and committed to what Jesus said and did so that, from now on, from Jesus onwards, our ideas of God and our response to God have to be shaped and controlled by what Jesus reveals to us of God in preference to revelation from any other source. Jesus Christ was the representative of God, yes: but even more, God was in Christ. The subject matter of this chapter is in the end more important than the subject of the last, because this takes him out of his own period of history and brings him right into the middle of ours.

God

Why did not the first Christians simply call Jesus God and worship Him only? Would not it have solved so much confusion and debate in later centuries if they had? Would it

not have matched the yearnings of ordinary Christians with
the most rigorous of intellectual demands for the unity and
integrity of God and so produced a faith that could stand
simply and clearly for the one God whose name is Jesus? One
could perhaps speculate that their reluctance to do this was
merely a hangover from their Jewish past, with its tremendous
emphasis on the oneness and indivisibility of God ('Hear, O
Israel, the Lord your God is one Lord') and that they were
horrified by the ease with which their pagan neighbours were
ready to see gods and goddesses everywhere. But this
speculation must give way before the one obvious reason why
the first Christians did not simply call Jesus God in that
simple way: the whole attitude of Jesus himself prevented it.
Always he had prayed to God, sought strength from Him,
dared to believe in Him; he had taught his disciples to pray to
God and call Him 'Father' and that was not just for them, it
was for himself also. He did not seek to persuade his disciples
to worship him, but God as he did himself. With that example
alive in their memories they just could not have maintained
that Jesus wanted them to worship him all the time really or
that he was the same as the Father.

Israel's own ideas about God had developed over the
centuries from positions not all that different from their
neighbours; they were convinced that Yahweh was their God,
their protector, lawgiver and saviour and that he was a
jealous god who would not allow them to give any of their
loyalty to any other of the powers, forces or gods that were
about in the world, particularly not to the gods of other
nations. But later, in the classic period of Hebrew thought,
when most of the Old Testament was written down in the
form we now have it, it was realized that there could only be
one creator and saviour God in the whole universe; and with
amazing boldness their later prophets declaimed that this God
was Yahweh, and that Israel thus stood in a favoured position
before all the other nations of the world, and all the other
so-called gods, even the gods of their mighty Babylonian
conquerors, were only figments of the imagination, mere
puffs of smoke. Reeling before the immensity thus perceived

for their God, Yahweh, the Hebrews were reluctant to think of Him in the intimate way they had before, moving among them, talking to them, getting angry with them and yearning for them and they became more conscious of His transcendant majesty and His otherness from anything that He had created; so great was His separateness from mortals that He was directly involved in the world through intermediaries such as the spirit, angels, wisdom or the word. These intermediaries however were aspects of God Himself; the important distinction for all Hebrew thought between God and man was not being broken; they were facets of God's own activity, his children, his messengers, his effective voices and they worked upon man enabling specially chosen and endowed men and women to do great things for God and become his prophets, his anointed ones and his sons and, at the appointed time, they would enable *the* Anointed One, *the* Son to bring in the kingdom.

During the century or so before Jesus, however, Judaism was surrounded and permeated by the Hellenistic culture which did not work with such a clear idea of the difference between the creator and His creation. Although the ultimate God was thought of intellectually as definable only by negatives, – infinite, ineffable, impassive, unchangeable – there was thought to be a whole hierarchy of beings between God and the world where, in the various gradations and permeations the qualities of divinity and humanity become intermingled. This is the world which the early Christians lived in and in which they had to find the words to express their new faith; their own background was in the classic Judaism, and their memories were of a Jesus who lived and spoke entirely in a Jewish world, but the language and thought forms in which they had to proclaim, defend and work out their faith were Greek and the categories of Hellenistic thinking were there to be used. St Paul and the Epistle to the Hebrews provide examples of this blending of Hebrew and Hellenistic language but probably the most profound work in the New Testament that does this is St John's Gospel. The use of the word *theos* God in the Fourth

Gospel illustrates this; in the first verse of the Gospel the Word, *Logos,* is declared to be both *with God* and *God,* although it is not as direct as it sounds in English since there *theos* has not got the definite article as one would expect if it was a noun – hence the paraphrases of many translations instead of 'and the word was God' (eg NEB 'and what the Word was, God was'; GNMM 'he was the same as God') and many commentators point out that identification between the Word and God is not meant; then in *20.28* Thomas uses the Old Testament confession 'My Lord and my God' to proclaim his faith in the risen Christ; but in *10.34* the Scriptures are quoted to prove that *men* can properly be called *theoi,* gods, and if men are gods according to Scripture then there is nothing outrageous in the claims being made for Jesus that he is God. Thus the word God is being claimed for the kind of close relationship with God which Hebrews of the classical period could never have used the word God for, and would never have thought that it was being used of anyone other than a human being. The very Gospel that makes Jesus say 'I and my Father are one' is also the Gospel that has Jesus affirming his total subservience to the Father in all things. The readiness to conceive of a plurality of beings and the gradations in the meaning of the word God are there for all to see.

This language was literally a Godsend to the early Church; it enabled it to talk of the risen Jesus as being in association with God, as being a mediator between God and man, as being the one through whom God had effected salvation, as being one who could properly be worshipped and adored, without raising the issue: was he, is he, God or man; worship could properly be offered because it was ultimately directed not at Jesus but at the God who had vindicated and exalted him. The word 'Son' could still be used, as it was throughout the Old and New Testaments, as a word about *relationship to God*; it denoted one who was loved and chosen and destined for inheritance by his Father and one who loved and was obedient to his Father; it did not carry with it the implication of being *generically one* with the Father, one in being and nature, but rather one in will and purpose, as in St John's Gospel. But once the ontological question was asked: 'is he God or man?' then the usefulness of this language is impaired.

In the 4th century AD, however, Arius asked this question and the Christian world could never be the same again[9]; he felt he had to draw the line between God and man between God and the Son – God must be God and the only creator, nothing must threaten that; everything else, everyone else, including the Son must therefore derive their being from God; certainly the Son was the first born of all creation, and thus superior in status to everything else but he must be on the creation side of this great divide. Most of the Christian bishops and teachers were outraged at this, and the Council of Nicaea in 325 AD firmly drew the line higher up so that the Father and the Son were God; the Son still derived his being from the Father but was begotten, not created, and this word was chosen because it was regarded as keeping the Son on the God side of the great divide. Now I do not have to argue who was right, Arius or Athanasius who led the opposition, or whether either of them could be either right or wrong; Arius had a good deal more Biblical truth on his side than has been traditionally acknowledged but Athanasius was clearly running more nearly to the tide of popular devotion. My point is that the mere raising of the question challenged most of the Christological language that had been used from the New Testament times to Nicaea on the issue that it had not, on the whole, had to be clear about before.

The Consequences of Identifying The Son with The Word

Thus the Nicene declaration created this great problem for Christology; the word Son was now being used, not for *Jesus in his relationship with the Father*, but for *that aspect or activity of God concerned with His relationship with the world right through from the creation onwards*; what we know as the Word, or the Spirit or the Wisdom of God was now *identified* with the Son who was Jesus so that the Son did not begin with Jesus, as all the New Testament language implied. Different passages of the New Testament suggest that the word Son became appropriate for Jesus at different moments: *Romans 1.4* suggests it was at the resurrection:

> the gospel concerning his Son, who was descended from David according to the flesh and designated Son of God in power according to the spirit of holiness by his resurrection from the dead

whereas it was at his baptism by John in the Jordan as the heavenly voice in the original Lukan version, 3.22, implies: '*This is my beloved Son; this day have I begotten him*' or at his conception in the womb of Mary as Christians have often thought although the future tenses of *Luke 1.32 and 35* do not necessarily mean that:

> he will be called the Son of the Most High; the child to be born will be called holy, the Son of God.

But now, in the post-Nicaean Christian world, it is asserted that the Father-Son relationship is eternal but the trouble is that human minds cannot exercise the discipline to remember that eternity is *outside time* but continually want to imagine it as *time extended backwards and forwards*: they imagine eternity as everlastingness. So now when they hear the phrase 'God sent His Son into the world', Christians imagine not the breaking into our world of time and space by an eternal God so that His incarnate presence can have a filial relationship with Him whom he can call, in human language, Son, but what they imagine is the descent from another level of time and space of *an already existing being*. That is the problem that the Nicene declaration sets for Christology.

The problem was compounded in the period of the classical Christological discussions because everyone was convinced that this Son, now conceived of as already existing, pre-existent, must have, not only a nature, *physis* (a set of characteristics that set him apart from other beings and enabled one to classify him into a category of being), but also must be a distinct entity, must have a *hypostasis*. It was this that made the difference between just being an abstract idea and actually existing; to exist, every *physis* had to have an *hypostasis*, or to use the Latin terms in which all our Western thinking has been done, every *natura* or *substantia* has to have a *persona*.

Part of the complications of all this lies in the slightly different meanings that can be put on the same basic ideas when they appear in the words of different languages. Anyone who has done any translating, or indeed had to move in two different languages knows this problem. What the Christian theologians were trying to get at may seem quite reasonable in Greek – *physics & hypostasis* but altogether too concrete and precise in Latin *nature/substance & person*.

However, as we mentioned before, both the schools of Christian thinking about the Person of Christ at this time, the Antiochene and the Alexandrian, were in the East and were working in Greek. They both accepted the Nicaen starting point and so presupposed a pre-existent divine being who was distinct from God the Father yet of the same substance; his substance was his divine nature and his distinctiveness was his divine person.

The problem was that before you set yourself to give any account of the only being for which you had any evidence – the historical Jesus of Nazareth and the Risen Christ of Christian experience – you were already landed with a complete, self-sufficient divine being with his own character, nature and existence into which you had to place whatever you wanted to say about the historical Jesus and the Risen Christ. As we have already seen, the only thing the Antiochenes could do was to produce accounts that looked dangerously like a two-personed Christ – who in terms of his will must have been literally schizophrenic, in the original Greek sense of that word – and the only thing that the Alexandrians could do was to produce accounts that looked dangerously like an unhuman Christ – who in terms of his will functioned as God all the time and was only pretending to doubt, be afraid or not to know. To put it rather strongly, before anyone could give an account of the known Christ of historical evidence and personal experience, they had to fit him into an entirely hypothetical divine Person who made all their explanations unsatisfactory. The Chalcedonian compromise was a magnificent attempt to provide a framework in which a believable account of the real Christ could be given; those who think the Holy Spirit was not only guiding the church into the best thing then possible but also into a permanent definition which is still the best thing possible, will defend the Chalcedonian formula still. There are those who do still argue that the basic framework of Chalcedon is still the best we have got and any modification has more disadvantages than otherwise.[10] But the last chapter was intended to show why the majority of modern theologians are dissatisfied by Chalcedon's provision for the humanity of Christ; and this one is trying to show why many modern theologians feel that its provision for the divinity of Christ starts from a point of view we no longer have to start with.

The Divine Nature of The Son

Let us look a little closer at what we could mean by the divine nature. We saw earlier that the Greeks maintained that since it was impossible with merely human language to describe God, you could only say what he was not – He was definable only by negatives like ineffable, indivisible, and unknowable. The one they felt was most important was *unchangeable*; God must be totally reliable, always the same. Their word for it was 'without passion' in the sense that God would not be affected by events, he was unmoved and moveable. But of course passion also means suffering, and thus the idea of God's impassivity also carries with it the idea that he cannot suffer. Now when this conception of the divine nature is applied to the divine nature of Christ you can see the difficulties that are going to emerge. How could God be in any way affected by what happened to Jesus if an essential aspect of His nature was unchangeableness? If the Chalcedonian Christ was one person who in his human nature suffered and died, could you say that *he* suffered and died? No,

because then *he* would have done that which he could not do
without denying his divine nature. So he must have 'suffered
impassively' said some of the Fathers. This is not Stoic
idealism, feeling offended at a Jesus who is reported to have
shrunk from death in the garden of Gethsamane and uttered a
loud cry on the cross; it is the consequence of trying to do
justice to a Jesus who is, and who remains throughout his
earthly life as well as his resurrection life, essentially a person
of the Godhead with all the characteristics that are essential to
Godhead retained. If God must be unchangeable and impassive, then Christ must be unchangeable and impassive *as well
as* the opposites of these things that belong to his human
nature. Poetic piety and a lot of traditional devotion can hold
these two together: there is a hymn in the English Hymnal (no
29) by H.R.Bramley that revels in this paradox of opposites:

> A Babe on the breast of a Maiden he lies
> Yet sits with the Father on high in the skies;
> Before him their faces the Seraphim hide
> While Joseph stands waiting, unscared, by his side.
> O wonder of wonders, which none can unfold;
> The Ancient of Days is an hour or two old;

and so on. Now this is romantic and beautiful in a strange
way; in one sense it forces us to revise our ideas of God by
presenting us with an Almighty Creator who can also exist as
a helpless baby and in that way it is doing the crucial job that
must be done, the complete reversal of our ideas about God
once we accept that Jesus is God for us. But fundamentally
this sort of poetry is only dealing in paradox and is totally
unsatisfactory as a way of understanding how Jesus could be.
The phrase 'he suffered impassively' is doing exactly the same
thing although it is much more unsatisfactory, devotionally
and historically.

Self-Emptying

One possibility that was much investigated at the beginning of
this century was the idea that the Word divested himself of

some of his divine characteristics to enable a proper incarnation to take place. The idea takes its inspiration from the early Christian hymn quoted by Paul in *Philip. 2.6–11* as he urges Christians to have the same mind among themselves as they have in Christ Jesus:

> who, though he was in the form of God, did not count equality with God a thing to be grasped, but emptied himself, taking the form of a servant, being born in the likeness of men. And being found in human form he humbled himself and became obedient unto death, even death on a cross. Therefore God has highly exalted him and bestowed on him the name which is above every name, that at the name of Jesus every knee should bow ... and every tongue confess that Jesus Christ is Lord.

These fascinating verses provide us with probably the best example of the earliest form of New Testament Christology where Jesus from a lowly state in which man-language is appropriate is exalted by God at the resurrection/ascension to a state where God-language is appropriate; they are clearly intended to draw a stark contrast between Jesus and Adam, both of whom were in the form or image of God; but while Adam counted equality with God a thing to be grasped at, Jesus emptied himself and was born as man. Were we studying New Testament Christology in greater detail we would have to spend much time on this passage, but the reason for referring to it now is because of the word 'he emptied himself'; the Greek word used is *ekenosen* from which the 'kenotic' theory, concerning the 'kenosis', or 'self-emptying' of the divine person, derives its name, although the outworkings of the idea go far beyond what anyone would argue was in the mind of Paul.

The best known versions of this theory suggest that the Word, while keeping those attributes which are essential to the Deity itself, without which God would not be God, such as love, justice, goodness *etc*, voluntarily gave up or emptied himself of those attributes which were in some sense relative because they referred to his relation with the world and therefore would not exist if there were no world; omnipotence, omnipresence and omniscience are examples. If the Word gave up being able to do anything in the world, to be anywhere and to know everything about the world then you can see that there is a greater chance that such a divine person could more easily function as the expression of a human nature. The great advantage of this idea, apart from trying to provide a way in which the Chalcedonian Christ could more easily be human, is that it asserts that the very revelation of God that we receive in Christ is of a God who is self-naughting: not an Almighty God but a self-emptying God, who chooses to be known not in glory and power but in humiliation and shame, with all the consequences that this has for those who want to please God or make themselves like Him; in this the theory elaborates the moral emphasis which is the point of the Philippians passage.

But as a doctrinal development of Chalcedon it is less successful; at any rate, the idea has not attracted much support from Anglican theologians recently, although it is to be found among Eastern Orthodox writers quite frequently now. William Temple voiced a very simple objection; 'to say that the Creative Word was so self-emptied as to have no being except in the Infant Jesus, is to assert that for a certain period the history of the world was let loose from the control of the Creative Word.[11] There are certainly difficulties about the idea of God giving up his relational qualities for since there is a world, how could God give up all his attributes that relate to the world? The presence of the Holy Spirit, if it (he/she?) is not incarnate too, – and that is not such an absurd idea as it might seem, for most of the New Testament language about Spirit relates her very closely to Jesus – may perhaps provide a being who can carry on these functions in the 'absence' of the Word, but you can see that if we start dividing up tasks among the different aspects of the Godhead we have reached the very boundaries of what Trinitarian language can do for us; that is pressing the imagery too far.

Another objection to the kenotic theory is that it finds

extreme difficulty in accounting for the post-resurrection Christ – is he still renouncing his divine powers? Actually of course the Chalcedonian Christ fits much more easily to the post-resurrection Christ, the Christ of the Fourth Gospel, and its weaknesses are apparent when we are trying to think of Jesus of Nazareth. The kenotic theory works best as long as we are thinking only of the incarnate Word; it is less easy to see how it helps after the exaltation, unless, and this is a point I think we must come back to again and again, we are prepared to let go our philosophically formed ideas about God and *reshape* them working solely from what Jesus shows us about God. The kenotic theory will have to be given further attention; the ecumenical dialogue will see to that.

A 'Chalcedonian Reversal'?

I want now to refer briefly to some ideas in P.Schoonenberg's book *The Christ*, because he takes up the assertion that many of the Christological problems have been caused by positing a divine Son *before* the birth of the Son Jesus Christ. He insists that the primary source of all this language must be the Incarnate Christ and that there are great dangers in allowing our ideas of a pre-existent Son to control what we say of the Incarnate Word, eg:

> What is said of the pre-existent divine person can never nullify this one and human person. We must then never conceive the divine person as added to the man Jesus in such a way that Christ would no longer be one, or no longer man. But what does this mean? No Trinity and no God-man? On the contrary, as we shall see.
>
> Where God's Trinity, and especially the divine person of the Word are concerned, we must first establish that we do not know the Trinity outside its revelation, and that this revelation occurs in the Word that is flesh and in the Spirit which is poured out ... Outside this revelation we do not know it.[12]

He casts doubt over all talk of a pre-existent Son except insofar as it is the pre-existence of the only Son we know, that is Jesus Christ and this, if there is such, is when God speaks many times and in many ways to the fathers; it is not a different or additional existence to the activity of the Word that the Fourth Gospel and Hebrews speak of in their first chapters; it is the dealings that God had with the world before the incarnation when the distinction between Father and Son does not mean anything, eg:

> Let it be further noted that the positing of the same personal distinction between Father and Son 'before' the becoming man as afterwards, gives to the message that 'God has sent his Son' the tinge of: he did not come himself, which is not in agreement with Jesus' words in John, that in him is the Father.[13]

The only way, insists Schoonenberg, that we know the divine person that is Christ is in the incarnate Jesus who is a divine-human person. Recall the 'enhypostasia' of Leontius of Byzantium (page 62) where he tried to do justice to the human person (hypostasis) of Jesus by suggesting that the one divine person of the Incarnate One includes in it all that is necessary for giving expression to the human person as well. Schoonenberg offers the exact opposite which he calls a reversal of the Chalcedonian pattern: it is the divine nature which is without an hypostasis, he suggests; the Word's divine nature expresses itself wholly in the person of the human nature; Chalcedon is preserved in that it is one person and two natures, but instead of a divine person with a divine nature taking to himself a complete human nature also, Schoonenberg suggests that what happens in the incarnation is self-identification of the divine nature with a human person and this brings about, or one might say, introduces in God Himself a new person and thus, for the first time, it is possible to speak of a Father and Son relationship. You may feel that here justice is being done to all that really matters in the language about the self-emptying of God; He does not give up any powers or relationships but condescends to be expressed in and through a human person; He takes to Himself the man Jesus, through whom the divine nature is content to express itself.

Through this 'Christological humanism' Schoonenberg links the fulness of God in Christ to the fulness now possible for all human beings. Referring to the texts in Colossians where it is said that all the fulness of God dwells bodily in Christ (*1.19 & 2.9*) he says:

> This does not mean that Christ comes to stand on a lonely height, for the work of salvation is directed to men; 'you have come to fullness of life in him' (*Col. 2.10*), 'that you may be filled with all the fullness of God' (*Eph. 3.19*). The dwelling of God's fullness in Christ appears to be a terminal point . . . but in its own context it is rather a beginning and a point of departure. The Fullness of the Godhead, which previously had communicated itself only partially, dwells wholly in him in order that we are fulfilled 'with all the Fullness'.[14]

Conclusion

Here indeed is the point of all Christology: it is not to separate Jesus from the rest of mankind but to bring what he is, and what he has done and what he makes known, to the rest of mankind; Christology has to bring the terms, the notions of God and man closer together if those are the terms it is having to work with. Athanasius[15] put it boldly when he wrote that the Word became man in order to make us gods. In this he was only following up a phrase in *2 Peter 1.4* about us becoming partakers in the divine nature. There is here a feeling for a way of thinking by which divinity and humanity are not opposites but have come together. Perhaps we need another way of thinking about God; perhaps we do not have to do our Christology only in terms of God and man.

Many speakers, writers and thinkers about Christ over the centuries have made the point that to confess Jesus as Lord means that we have to think of God in a completely new way;

if Jesus is *God for us* then new qualities, virtues and attributes must dominate our ideas of God. J.Moltmann's book *The Crucified God* makes the point in its title, and Karl Barth's vast theological operation was conceived to try and start afresh with Jesus Christ as the touchstone for everything that was said. We have seen that many contemporary theologians think that some of the difficulties of Chalcedon stem from its working with ideas of God that derive from philosophical systems that we do not have to work with today. To finish with, I want to refer to an idea of God that may help us forward into the next stage.

I remember being tremendously impressed with Tillich's assertion about God when I first came across it that the last thing that anybody should say of God is that he exists; for to assert that God exists is to reduce him to the level of a being among other beings. Listen to this fighting talk from his *Systematic Theology*:[16]

> Thus the question of the existence of God can neither be asked nor answered. If asked . . . the answer – whether negative or affirmative – implicitly denies the nature of God. It is as atheistic to affirm the existence of God as it is to deny it. God is being itself, not *a* being.

In the light of this, another sort of Christology is needed and I think that it will be with the heady spirit of Tillich that the next chapter will begin.

6

Jesus: Prophet, Priest, King; the Way, the Truth, the Life

Introduction

Two things have been asserted in what has gone before: *first*, that the one sure historical fact that we have to begin with in any statement about Jesus is that he was a man and that the quite proper impulse to say more than human things about him should not lead us to deny that basic link with historical fact with which we start; and *second*, that the trouble with most of our concepts of God is that we feel we must imagine God as a being who actually exists somewhere and thus are landed with many difficulties in describing Jesus as both God and man. The challenge to think of God as 'the ground of being' or the 'power of being' – both phrases used by Tillich as he tries to get us to see the implications of the ancient view of God, long known to Christian philosophers, of God as subject not object, as not outside the being of the universe but the cause and sustainer of it and immanent in it. This of course is not pantheism because it is not asserted that all things are God but that nothing could be but for God. John Macquarrie, in the book which is a text book in most theological colleges, arguing much the same point writes about God as 'holy being' or Being, and he makes much use of the phrase 'letting-be' to express the creativity of such Being; he rejects phrases like 'the energy that permits beings to be' because the word 'energy' has too much the flavour of a physical force and thus brings us back into the world of particular beings.[17] We are now going to consider what Christology can look like with that view of God and man, such as the Biblical words prophet, priest, king, the Way, the Truth and the Life.

Essential Being Under the Conditions of Existence

One of the characteristics of Tillich's theological method is that, believing that the Christian Gospel is about the condition of all humanity and needs to be listened to by all cultures and races, he wants to find a way by which its universal application can be made immediately accessible to those who have not been brought up in the traditional story language of the Gospel. He seeks to match up the story language of theology with the abstract language of philosophy, believing that philosophical terms are neutral and universal and in a sense represent mankind's questions about man and the universe while the theological stories represent a kind of answer offered by the Christian Gospel. For example, he describes our awareness of being as of two kinds: *existential being* which is being as you and I actually experience it with all its frustrations and tensions and *essential being* which is the true and undistorted nature of things which always seem to lie beyond our actual experience of things. We so often know that things ought to be different, and could be, but they just are not; we can dream of a world where things 'work' but it seems to be only a dream. If this is put into the language of the Christian story, existence is the world as 'fallen'; essence is the world as God made it and means to be. But the condition is one that can be recognized without the theological language; the distinction is one that runs through all philosophical thinking; the frustrations of existence have been described most profoundly by the existentialists of our own century.

Tillich further elaborates this by enumerating some pairs of qualities which we usually experience in tension. Being as we actually know it is where such things as freedom and destiny, dynamics and form, individualization and participation are opposites, fighting against each other and frustrating each others' full realization. It helps to understand what Tillich means by these 'polarities' because the removal of the tensions between them is what he sees as the saving act which God in Christ performs for the whole human race; they form, in short, part of his Christology.

The first pair is *freedom and destiny*; we are all conscious of an element of freedom in our lives, we can choose this or that and at times we feel that we are in control; but then we are also conscious of the power wielded over every aspect of life by circumstance, by the decisions of others and it seems that we are being rolled along inexorably towards a destiny we have had nothing to do with; destiny and freedom appear as opposites. Theologically, we cannot work out a satisfactory reconciliation between the free will we believe God gives us and the power of His over-riding Providence; predestination and free-will are seen as opposites, and not merely 'seen' as such, for this is more than just an intellectual exercise, it is a desperately real part of living as we know it.

The second pair is *dynamics and form*; we know we have a certain creativity within us, a dynamic to do and think great things; but we know also that the sheer physical difficulties of translating any of our ideas purely into action so often either prevents the idea from coming to expression or waters it down into banality. I might have an idea for a great oratorio, or of a great act of love and feel that I had got it in me and that it was not impractical, but over and over again the sheer technicalities of doing it, the structure of the way things are, will defeat me. 'A minister of the Word who writes about preaching' wrote R.E.C.Browne 'writes as a learner to other learners and like them he is haunted by the sermon that no one is great enough to preach'[18]; that is the tension between dynamics and form as we all know it in different ways.

Lastly *individualization and participation*; we want to be ourselves, to be free to develop our own characters, not in isolation from other people but with them, sharing and interacting with them; yet under the conditions of existence living in community seems to require suppression of one's individuality, the sacrifice of oneself for the greater good of all; why cannot you be yourself as well as participate fully in the lives of your fellow human beings; why are individualization and participation continually at odds with each other? St Paul, after dictating a whole chapter about these tensions of existence in terms of doing good and evil cries out 'Who will deliver me from the body of this death?' (*Romans 7.24*).

When Christians confess Jesus as the Christ, says Tillich, and acknowledge that in some way he has brought salvation, wholeness, into the world, – the New Being in his terminology – they are affirming that in Jesus essential manhood has appeared under the conditions of existence; in him the polarities are not opposites but are reconciled. He was free at every point; his will was to fulfil the destiny laid down for him by his Father; his dynamic power found a way of working within the structure of the world as he found it and while being most truly himself he could be hailed as the man who lived 'for others'.

The New Being

Now it is important to see that Tillich at this point is not thinking here principally about the historic Jesus; that Jesus of Nazareth was a new kind of person in this way is not doubted but the *saving* aspect of Jesus comes in when Christians confess him as lord and saviour. Tillich writes:

> without this reception the Christ would not have been the Christ, namely the manifestation of the New Being in time and space. If Jesus had not impressed himself as the Christ on his disciples and through them upon all following generations, the man who is called Jesus of Nazareth would perhaps be remembered as an historically and religiously important person ... He could then have been a prophetic anticipation of the New Being, but not the final manifestation of the New Being itself. The receptive side of the Christian event is as important as the factual side.[19]

Two things are absolutely crucial here. One is that the Risen Christ is being made the subject of Christology rather than Jesus of Nazareth; or rather that it is the Risen Christ that compels us towards a different sort of Christology and where the primary focus must be. The Risen Christ is Jesus as experienced by two thousand years of believers; the Body of Christ is the risen body into which believers are gradually being incorporated and which they find to be the source and power of a new sort of being. The second is that who Jesus is cannot be separated from what Jesus does; whenever these two themes, the Person of Christ and the Work of Christ are pursued independently then there is a danger that the power of the analogies being used to explicate the one theme will be unchecked by the analogies used in the other; and both are liable to go wrong if they are not linked to what happens in and to us, to believers. The Person of Christ can be so described that he is separated from us as a different kind of being without any real humanity and the Work of Christ can be described as a transaction between two different Persons of the Godhead; and then, belatedly, the attempt has to be made to interest us human beings in this different being and this reputed transaction. Whereas, if what has been said just now is true, what happens to believers is part of what Jesus does and thus, consequently, part of who he is.

The Focus of Being

Macquarrie, who uses language very similar to Tillich, describes Jesus as the 'symbol' of Being; here he is using the word 'symbol' in the same sense as Tillich does, meaning, not something merely standing for something else – 'symbolizing' it but not being it – but meaning by symbol something in which the thing symbolized is not only present but also manifests itself so that others can see it and recognize it. In Jesus, in other words, the essential nature of our being is not only present but also apparent, not only arrived but also manifested, and we celebrate this by Advent and Epiphany. A parallel phrase that Macquarrie uses in this context is 'focus' of Being:

> The event of Jesus Christ is for Christian faith the supreme miracle, the high tide of God's providential

activity. As such, it focuses the presence and activity which are indeed everywhere, but of which we remain unaware until such a focusing occurs, and the 'mystery hidden for ages' is made 'manifest'. Jesus Christ then is the focus where the mystery of Being is disclosed.[20]

Here too, in Macquarrie as in Tillich, we have the harnessing of existential language to the historical so that both can be understood in the light of each other; this is not just an exercise in communication, trying to find a way in which the truths of Christian revelation can be made understandable to those not brought up in its traditions; it recognizes that the truths of the Christian revelation need to be confronted by the understanding of existence that we have today because both will be affected, and thus changed to some extent, by each other. A way in which this can happen is shown in this quotation from Macquarrie where the God-manhood of Christ is interpreted as his creative Being and his creaturely being:

> God is absolute letting-be, and letting be is the ontological foundation of love. Letting-be is also self-giving or self-spending, so that God's creative work is a work of love and self-giving, into which he has put himself. Insofar as created beings themselves manifest creativity, love, self-giving, they tend to be like God. This self-giving is supremely manifested in the particular being, Jesus Christ . . . Just as there is a self-emptying, or *kenosis*, of God as he pours out Being, so Christ empties himself in the life that is portrayed in the gospels. But how could this relative self-emptying in a finite particular being manifest the absolute letting-be of God? To this, it must be replied that death is the one absolute in human life. By this is meant not just the moment of physical death, but the taking up of death into life so that existence itself becomes a being-towards-death. Christ's self-giving, his love, or letting-be, becomes complete and absolute in the accepting of the cross.

Selfhood passes into Christhood, the human Jesus
becomes the Christ of faith ... And what we see in
Christ is the destiny that God has set before humanity;
Christ is the first-fruits, but the Christian hope is that 'in
Christ' God will bring all men to God-manhood.[21]

A Breather Before Further Advance

I know that this sort of language and this concentrated kind
of argument is not easy; but I believe it to be worth the effort
because this line of thinking is not just verbal cleverness but
does actually get us out of some of the God-man difficulties
we have seen in the two previous chapters and, moreover,
puts forward an idea of God that is just as alive and dynamic
in a different sense as the one we are moving away from. It is
reported that a recent small child's prayer was 'I am sorry for
you, dear God, up there in heaven, while I am down here in
the real world'; *O sancta simplicitas*! Out of the mouths of
babes and sucklings ...!

In the 1960s we heard much about the 'death of God'
which was being talked about among theologians; what most
of them were discussing was not atheism but what theology
looks like if you abandon the notion of God as a particular
being out there. What many of them meant was the death of
the concept of God that could be rejected and the renewal of
the concept of God that made Him inescapably involved in
every reality. Nor was the essay collection entitled *The Myth
of God Incarnate* suggesting the abandoning of the idea of the
Incarnation altogether – after all some of them meant by
'myth' much the same as Macquarrie and Tillich mean by
'symbol'; what they were investigating was precisely the
shape of Christology in its various historical manifestations.
The discussion that this book called forth constitutes the most
profound treatment of Christology that this country has seen
for many decades and is essential reading for anyone wishing
to pursue these matters further.

Analogies not Definitions

One of the most crucial developments in recent times about the nature of religious language has been the realization that since the subject of religious language is beyond human experience but that language can only be based on human experience, then religious language is essentially *analogous* or symbolical. We cannot analyse, define or encapsulate God in our language but we can make stabs towards him by pictures, similes and poetic speech; 'He is like this, and this, and this' each word adding something to the total picture but also having its full force diminished by the existence of the others. This point could not be better made than by the following hymn verse[22]:

> Jesus! my Shepherd, Husband, Friend,
> My Prophet, Priest, and King
> My Lord, my Life, my Way, my End,
> Accept the praise I bring

When we look at these various titles, Shepherd, Prophet, Priest, King and Lord probably go into one group as well attested and familiar New Testament titles; all of them have one or more than one meaning in the New Testament which need to be explained and the titles have to be justified as relevant to Christ; inevitably each title is only partially applicable to Christ and no one title has such pre-eminence that it should be allowed to control interpretation. Three of them, Prophet, Priest and King, became the bearers of much official Christology in classical Protestant dogmatics[23] and we may start with them.

Prophet. This is an ordinary word by which some of Jesus' Jewish contemporaries were able to explain him to themselves as a man inspired by God to speak out boldly declaring God's truth in a specific context. In first century Palestine there was an additional nuance to this word, that we do not always pick up in that in Jesus' day the spirit of prophecy was regarded as being dead; it was only to be revived again in the last days, so to designate Jesus as a prophet was something out of the ordinary; he was the Prophet who was to come into the world, the proclaimer and introducer of the Kingdom itself. After the first few years this title was not much used by Christians of Jesus, being overshadowed by weightier words, but it stands in the Christian tradition for his revelatory work as the fulfilment of the Old Testament. In our own times the title prophet has come alive again for many people who are uncertain whether they can accept other claims for him.

Priest. Never used in Judaism of Jesus since he was not of priestly family and appears never to have made any such claims himself; but the Letter to the Hebrews uses it, in a bold and daring analogy, to claim that Jesus means the total and absolute end of the Old Testament; the argument is that worship according to the Law of Moses was only a shadow of the real worship in heaven which has now been done permanently and once for all by Jesus. This is a daring analogy because it has to be stretched to its limits, since Jesus has to be both priest and victim. In tradition the title priest for Jesus has borne two important ideas; Jesus as mediator between man and God, mediator in intercession to God and in revelation to man and Jesus as sacrifice for sin. It has had a certain polemic character to it, particularly since the Reformation, affirming that Jesus supplies all that is needed of the priestly functions and therefore these are not appropriate for the ministers of the church. I doubt if the word means anything much to 20th century worshippers and presume it is not any longer in the forefront of our Christological armoury.

King. God of course is the ultimate king of Israel and of the world; his kingdom is regarded as having been introduced and established by Jesus, but it is primarily God's kingdom. But this is complicated by the fact that the Messiah was to be a son of King David and thus would reintroduce the glories of his kingship in the new age; so Jesus is called King not just sarcastically or prophetically or reportedly but in a few places in the New Testament of his present universal rule (*1 Cor.*

15.24f, Col. 1.13, 1 Pet. 1.11 and several references in *Revelation*). Jesus as king has however been a very popular theme throughout the whole history of the Church and a glance at any hymn book will show how common it is for 20th century Christians to acknowledge Jesus by that word. King of our hearts; yes, we know what that means; but king of the Church, yes, acknowledged as such and we try to make him such; but king of the world, what on earth does that mean? In the last century or so the imagery of kingship has taken a sore battering, and I wonder how long it will be before Christians realize that for many people kingship means either tyranny (that is has always meant) or, and this is comparatively new, authority that is totally depotentiated, rule only in name, ceremonial and tongue-in-the-cheek kind of power when all real authority is held elsewhere and kingship is kept on for old time's sake and for certain minor, if real advantages, that kingship gives. Is this what we want the kingship of Christ to mean?

To come back to Newton's hymn: the second group of titles is to me astonishingly innovative and daring for the 18th century but perhaps I am only showing my ignorance of the period: 'Husband, Friend'. God as the husband of Israel has support in the Old Testament but this putting forward of Jesus in a relationship that must mean most to women is a very good example of what we must keep doing in Christology, so that the new ideas contained in new analogies can be checked and modified by the total picture but also make their own contribution to a new understanding and a renewed commitment. 'Friend' too is interesting; Jesus calls his disciples his friends but to put it the other way round is charming and wholly appropriate; this is another good example of how an analogy can make its own contribution, bolstered up by the company it keeps. D.M.Baillie reported on a Christology centering on the word 'Leader' propounded by Karl Heim, but that it suffers from the same disadvantages as the word 'king' and, as near to the Second World War as that, the idea of Jesus as *Führer* was not likely to commend itself.

In the third category in Newton's hymn we are faced by impersonal and abstract nouns, 'my Life, my Way, my End'. The first two come from the trio in *John 14.6* where the evangelist makes Jesus say 'I am the way and the truth and the life; no one comes to the Father but by me'. John uses many such words, impersonal analogies like Bread, Way, and Door and abstract nouns like Truth and Life, his point being that the abstract aspects of God himself have been made concrete, incarnated, in Jesus so that we can hear, touch and see them 'in the flesh' in the two senses that this has in the gospel: the historic fact of his being a man and the experiential fact of his risen presence in a new kind of body. The ultimacy of God must be preserved at all costs in our understanding of these nouns and therefore we must say the same sort of things about them as we have seen we must say about the Godhead of Jesus. Just as he is not God pure and simple, but Son of God, image of God *etc* so he is not Truth or Life pure and simple, for the only truth or life that he has and that he can communicate to us is God's truth and life, just as the only divinity he has comes from God his Father. It is because of his functions in our corporate experience that he is God for us, and in these practical senses therefore he is also truth and life for us. But I have also argued that because the truth and life of God is not something additional to being as we know it but is the very ground of our being, undistorted by the frustrations of existence, and thus the true, essential nature of being, which for us humans is humanity, then it follows that when the life and truth that is God is made known to us, as we believe it is in Jesus, then he is not merely communicating something to us but is what he is communicating.

Man's Will and God's Will

So again we have reached the heart of Christology: the Godness of Christ is not added to his humanity but is in the very quality and nature of his humanity, which broke the mould of our humanity and made him different from us in such a way that we could become what he is. It is because he is like us in all things except sin that it is at the actual point of difference that we see in him the essential character of our own real being; the point at which one who is like us actually achieves, in conditions such as we live in, freedom to be himself and at the same time wholly open to others and able to give new life and hope to others. 20th century Christians have got to see this in terms of Jesus' will, for it is in psychological terms, and not only in ontological or mythological ones, that we must see how Jesus as the Christ can make us whole, can save us.

In this sense the Gethsamane prayer is the most Christologically important passage in the New Testament 'Father, if You are willing, remove this cup from me; nevertheless not my will but Yours be done' (*Luke 22.42*). How can it actually be that the will to do what is good in us be strengthened to overcome the will to evil; how can our will be attracted by what is good so that we *want to do what is good*? That surely is the saved state as the 20th century Christian can understand and accept it. The paradox of grace is that as and when man turns his will towards God, then he knows that it is God working in him; 'I laboured more abundantly than they all, yet not I, but the grace of God which was with me' (*1 Cor. 15.10*). Many decades ago, D.M.Baillie suggested[24] that this was our best clue to how the Incarnation actually worked in Jesus since this is the point at which his work touches us. He suggested that we Christians still have our bodies and wills and yet confess that God has wrought everything good in us; this paradox in its fragmentary form in our own experience could therefore be the best clue we can have to the manner of the perfect union of God and man in the Incarnate One, which is the source of our experience. J.MacIntyre thinks that the Church has not paid nearly enough attention to the relation of our wills to Christ and his Spirit. When discussing the relevance of the psychological model to Christology and the doctrine of the Holy Spirit, he writes:

Many accounts of the Holy Spirit and his work stop short of the point where the issues for our day really occur – the point of his involvement in the decisions, the wills, the emotions, the cognitions, attitudes, character reactions of ordinary men and women . . . The relation of the human will to the Holy Spirit has been so enveloped in mystery that it has been left to extra-ecclesiastical groups like Alcoholics Anonymous to create a structure of moral recovery which has its ultimate foundations in the resources of the Christian faith. For this same reason, this silence concerning the relation of the Holy Spirit to the psyche of the human being, we have failed to provide our people with adequate doctrinal instruction because we do not possess the adequate psychological scaffolding with which to erect a devotional structure.[25]

Perhaps those from the traditions of Protestant and Catholic spirituality would maintain that more has been worked out than MacIntyre allows. As our knowledge of personality develops, and we learn more about self-consciousness and the unconscious I am sure that Christology will have new tools to work with and we can come to new understandings of what it meant to be that supreme person Jesus whom we call Christ.

What we know already however is that the voice of the church throughout all the centuries has affirmed that the only way it knows for us to have this total freedom of the human will, when what we want is gloriously what is good not only for us, but also for our fellow human beings and for all the created universe, is for us to become *in Christ*, that is, outwardly committed to him – in baptism, communion, speaking up for and practising Christ-like actions – and inwardly committed to him – in prayer and resolution. If doing that does make us gradually more integrated personalities, more whole human beings, then our confession of Jesus as 'God for us' is vindicated; and if not, then a question mark is placed against our Christological confession insofar as it is about what Christ is now. For the assertions about his being are consequences of his function and if he does not make us whole he is not what we say he is. The Person and the Work of Christ are inextricably bound together, but it is the latter that is prior; what Christians have said about the Person of Christ has always been dependent upon what they have perceived to be his Work. I said 'insofar as our confession is about what Christ is now' advisedly, that there is a 'not yetness' that runs all the way through the New Testament and this brings me to my last point.

Being and Becoming

Ever since the nineteenth century it has been realized that we are not in a static world where things stay as they are and so can be defined for all time. Evolution and development are written into our understanding of every field, and Christian doctrine is no exception as any study of the development of credal statements over the centuries will show. 'Becoming' is as significant a word as 'being' and the description of the way things are moving, or developing, is as much an aspect of the description of truth as statements about what things are. This should carry no surprises for Christians for whom the eschatological dimension has been present from the beginning; we have always known that our sights are on the end of time, not just as the cessation of chronology but more as the full revelation of the purpose of the universe and the final triumph of God. If Jesus Christ is part of this, as we believe, then it follows that his full nature and work is yet to be revealed here on earth and yet to happen.

I have referred already to the work of Teilhard de Chardin where we are given, as I understand it, an imaginative glimpse – based on the movement of anthropology and biology – of Christ as the decisive moment in the course of the evolution of man, who facilitates this development towards mature, integrated manhood and thus is himself the End of the process, while still part of it. Now the movement of creation onwards will mean that Teilhard's scientific and philosophical arguments may well need changing, along with those of every other thinker who ever has been, but the vision of *the Christ who is yet to be* is authentic to the whole Christian tradition. For that very reason there must be an element of reverent expectation in our words about Jesus Christ; I have no wish to criticize here the easy familiarity with which some Christians talk about Jesus although I cannot share it, but I do ask that we recognize the danger which we all face of wishful thinking about Jesus, seeing him in the image that we want to see him in. We ought to prepare ourselves to be challenged by him to the very depths of our inmost being, not just our individual being but our corporate being in the developing universe of which we are part, because that is where we will be taken if we submit to him.

PART 3

Saying What We Believe

7

The Apostles' and Nicene Creeds

At the end of the last chapter we saw that believing in Jesus as our revelation from God could mean that in him we have a glimpse into the unknowable future; we see in him what God will do with and for man, and we see man fulfilling the purposes of God. So we place our trust in one who was a man like us, believe that he talked to us truly about God and declare our readiness to be guided and controlled by his Spirit so that we may be shaped into his likeness. So far in this book we have considered this person in whom we trust, who he is and what has been believed about him. However much we have stressed that Christian faith is trust in a person rather than belief about things, we have not been able to do without words; nor have we been able to ignore the words that Christians of the past have used to express the implications of believing in Jesus. In this broadest sense then 'faith' or 'belief' (and let us remember that these are identical concepts in the Greek language, the language of the New Testament and in which all the first Christian thinking was done) begins as an attitude of trust involving the whole person, mind and body, but the moment it is put into words, immediately the attempt is made to focus this trust for oneself or to communicate and share it with others then is born a confession, a creed, a 'symbolum'. In this broadest sense then, a creed is at the heart of any religion and you cannot have a faith without having also some words to define it, to communicate it and to express it.

For the theistic religions there is a one word creed that is the very foundation stone on which any and every credal edifice is built: 'I believe in God'. Perhaps that is enough; you have said it all. In one sense you have; but you have really got to go on from there if you are going to be clear for yourself what that means and if you are going to be able to help others to the same faith. There are three obvious directions in which this faith in God has to be articulated further: something more is needed to describe the nature and character of God, something about how we can know Him and something about the implications of this faith for us and our world.[1] Zoroastrians believe in God, in Zoroaster and that they are subject to God's laws as mediated by him. Jews would say much the same with Moses instead of Zoroaster as the chief prophet. Islam confesses that Allah is one and that Mohammed is his prophet. Perhaps the shortest Christian creed is belief in God as Father and Jesus as his Son.

It is this two-fold pattern that dominates the embryo credal passages that we find in the New Testament: 'for us there is one God, the Father; and there is One Lord, Jesus Christ, through whom all things come and through whom we exist' (*1 Corinthians 8.6*); 'Before God the source of all life and before Jesus Christ who spoke up as a witness for the truth in front of Pontius Pilate' (*1 Timothy 6.13*); 'there is only one God and only one mediator between God and mankind, himself a man, Jesus Christ who sacrificed himself as a ransom for all' (*1 Timothy 2.5*); 'eternal life is this: to know you the only true God and Jesus Christ whom you have sent' (*John 17.3*). God is defined as the one and only God, as the Father and as the one who raised Jesus; Jesus is defined as Son, as Lord, as Christ. 'Christ died for our sins in accordance with the scriptures, that he was buried,' (*1 Corinthians 15.4*) and *1 Peter 3.18–22* has a more developed passage through four verses rehearsing how Jesus died, descended to the dead, was raised, ascended, and sits now at God's right hand.

As well as these two types of embryo creeds in the New Testament (the dual 'Father and Son' and the intermediate where the second part is expanded) there is a third type, the triple form which also can be instanced in dozens of phrases from the New Testament but these four must suffice: 'There is a variety of gifts but always the same Spirit: there are all sorts of services to be done but always the same Lord: it is the same

God who is working in all of them' (*1 Corinthians 12.4*); 'it is God himself who assures us ... of our standing in Christ, marking us with his seal the Spirit that we carry in our hearts' (*2 Corinthians 1.21*); 'the grace of the Lord Jesus Christ, the love of God and the fellowship of the Holy Spirit be with you all' (*2 Corinthians 13.13*) and, the most obvious of all, (*Matthew 28.19*) 'make disciples of all the nations; baptize them in the name of the Father and of the Son and of the Holy Spirit'. Note here the connection between baptism and a formal three-fold invocation.

One observation before we leave the New Testament and look at what happened in the centuries that succeeded: the motives for producing these short formularies were many and varied; there was the spontaneous and creative exclamation of faith, there was the need to pass on the faith to others, to defend it against false teaching, and to express the faith in a liturgical context, as a witness to non-believers, as an apologetic to help non-believers to understand and come to belief, as a way of bringing differing Christians to realize their unity, as a test of orthodoxy – all the motives that led in later ages to the production of creeds, confessions, manifestos, articles, decrees and declarations were present as the first Christians struggled to find words for their new yet old experience of God. Is it not true that it is in the context of teaching others, or being faced with a word or idea that is not quite right, that we are challenged to say again and afresh what we believe and that in doing so we not only communicate something but learn a bit more ourselves? The phrase that has become part of us through repetition in worship suddenly becomes alive in a new way after reading a new book, after a particular conversation, after a memorable experience. External pressures and ordinary hum-drum requirements have contributed to the articulation of faith from the very beginning.

As we now move into the 2nd and 3rd centuries AD we pick up from the fairly scanty evidence we have various allusions to short summaries of the Christian faith and they show a continuation of the patterns we have seen in the New

Testament. Ignatius (*c.* 35–*c.* 107) has several quotations of the second type, brief rehearsals of the salient facts about Jesus of which just one must suffice here: 'our God Jesus Christ was conceived by Mary according to God's plan of the seed of David and of the Holy Spirit: who was born and was baptized that by His passion he might cleanse water' (*Ephesians 18.*2) while Justin (*c.*100–*c.*165) quotes mainly three-fold formulae 'we revere and worship Him and the Son, who came from Him and taught us these things and the prophetic Spirit' (*Apology* 1 6.2) and even more important we have the questions that were asked of the candidate for baptism in Justin's church: 'Do you believe in the Father and Lord God of the universe: do you believe in Jesus Christ our Saviour who was crucified under Pontius Pilate? Do you believe in the Holy Spirit, who spoke by the prophets?'[2] On receiving the three-fold yes from the candidate baptism took place. This is important because it is from these three questions at baptism which became almost universal throughout the church in the 3rd century, that the standard three-fold form of the classic creeds is derived. Baptism seems nearly always to have been associated with the Trinitarian formula, (after a brief time right at the beginning when we have baptism into the name of Jesus), and it is an interesting speculation that had other contexts been the dominant ones, we might have had more Binitarian creeds, because it was in the Father and the Son and their relationship that all the interest was focused in the 3rd, 4th, and even in the 5th centuries AD.

However it was not to be so and Trinitarian creeds very quickly prevailed. It was the training period leading up to baptism that provided the context for the gradual fixing of formulas of belief during the 3rd century among the churches of the west, with a growing uniformity, probably due to the influence of Rome. In the east there was a wider variety with each church, Constantinople, Antioch, Jerusalem, Ephesus, Alexandria, *etc.*, conscious of its own traditions and less willing to be uniform. What we are now going to look at are in formal senses the first clear texts we have of the baptismal creeds of the early church; but this does not mean necessarily what we mean by 'creeds'; they were a syllabus for instruction, they changed gradually according to the emphases that the teachers of the church felt they needed to bring out, they were liturgical in the sense that they were geared to the three questions that were going to be asked on the night of the baptism.

We look first at the texts[3] of the Roman baptismal formulae in the 3rd and 4th centuries AD in the text of Hippolytus from the Apostolic Tradition and the text of the Old Roman creed as quoted by Rufinus. We note first their similarity: the text at Rome was becoming fixed. We note also the terseness of the text and a certain matter-of-factness in its brisk statements; it all fits into the pattern of what we have seen already and the variants are not significant.

If we look at one of the comparable baptismal formulae in the eastern church (the one that is chosen, the creed of Caesarea from near Jerusalem, contributed to the construction of the Nicene creed,) there are two points of difference to note between these western and eastern baptismal creeds:

1. The eastern creed emphasizes the one God. This of course was believed in the west but there it was assumed without question. In the east it needed affirming explicitly because of the many more speculative questions that were being asked about the implications of believing in the divinity of Jesus.
2. In the east there is a much more careful stress on definition of the second person of the Trinity and exploring his relationship with the Father.

We return to the western church and look at the phrases that were added to the old Roman Creed before it became accepted generally in the west as the Baptismal Creed, used for other purposes, dignified with the name of 'The Apostles' Creed' and even provided with the ridiculous legend that the twelve apostles had written it, each contributing a phrase. The text of the Apostles' Creed as it became fixed in the west in the middle ages and as used in our English service books has several added phrases on which we can comment briefly:

1. 'Creator of heaven and earth' – This was always believed but it was not needed to be said when the idea was contained in the word 'Father', but later on Fatherhood was conceived more in terms of God's relation to Jesus and so the idea of God being the creator needed explicit proclamation. It had always been in the eastern creeds but now needed saying also in the west.

2. 'He was conceived by the Holy Spirit' – It became necessary to avoid misconceptions that Jesus was the son of the Holy Spirit and so two separate verbs were needed for the work of the Holy Spirit and the contribution of St Mary: 'conceived' and 'born'. This is a very delicate area and these phrases represent moves to distinguish the roles of the two in the begetting of Jesus.

3. 'Suffered' – This is simply a growing emphasis on the suffering of Jesus as itself redemptive.

4. 'He descended to the dead' – This is probably the place of the dead, the ancient idea appearing in the New Testament (*1 Peter 3:18*: 'in the spirit he went to preach to the spirits in prison') that those who had lived before Christ should have the opportunity to hear and respond to the Gospel of Redemption.

5. 'Catholic' – The assertion of the universality of the church over and against the growing number of sects.

6. 'The communion of saints' – The question here is the word 'sanctorum' masculine or neuter? It is probably the former and therefore this phrase refers to the fellowship between all those who are sanctified by Christ now and previously, though some commentators in early days interpreted saints more narrowly as those distinguished from amongst their fellows by their holiness. It is less likely that the

word 'sanctorum' is neuter and refers to the fellowship of the sacraments.

7. 'and the life everlasting' – a further emphasis on the implications of the word 'resurrection'.

With the beginning of the 4th century, a new situation emerges for the Church. Constantine was the Emperor and Christianity was declared to be the official religion of the whole world. Now the visible unity of the church mattered more, both to the church itself and to the state. So summaries of what the church believed were no longer only important as teaching frameworks for the church itself or telling interested inquirers what the church believed; they began to be needed as the basis of the constitution of an institution, as the title deeds and the bond of unity. So when Constantine called the Council of Nicaea in 325 it was mainly to get the church to settle its differences; for the first time there was state pressure on the church to settle its doctrinal differences, or at least if it could not do that, and this is a typical political view, to get a formula to which all parties could consent and thus preserve unity. The cause of difference was the considerable uncertainty in the more speculative Greek speaking east – it was not such an issue in the more matter of fact Latin speaking west – as to how you could preserve any kind of belief in one God if you were busy saying that Jesus was also the eternal God alongside the Father. It was focused at the beginning of the 4th century on the teachings of Arius who thought he could preserve the unity of the Godhead and be faithful to the New Testament itself by maintaining that Jesus was the head of all creation as a creature not as a creator. He was indeed a perfect creature, was properly called Word and Son of God but not the source of all life himself, not the one through whom all things were made. Now when Eusebius of Caesarea came forward with the baptismal creed of his own church it was hailed as an expression of the true faith; but the Arian party also accepted it for they were able to offer explanations of all the phrases; Jesus was 'God from God' but not in the full sense; he could be called God because of his mediatorial role; and they liked the phrase from Colossians 1:15 that came in the creed; 'first begotten of all creation' because it expressed exactly what they taught and proved they were saying what St Paul said. So other phrases were introduced by the Council of Nicaea specifically to exclude the teaching of the Arians:

1. 'true God from true God'; this counteracted what the Arians said about the phrase 'God from God'.

2. 'not made'; this was inescapably precise.

3. and, the most famous phrase of all, 'one in Being with the Father'; (the *homoousion*). This too was inescapable; but almost everyone was reluctant to agree to it for it brought in a non-Scriptural idea, the Greek philosophic term 'ousia', to try and make the point. What were you up to when you did this? Was it not dangerous ground? The danger becomes apparent when *ousia* is translated *substantia* (substance), and all kinds of other ideas tend to come with it. The Fathers were worried about it at Nicaea and all through the 4th century and we are still not happy with the word in the 20th century; on the whole their intentions were clear and most of us would sympathize with them, but we have to recognize that the word *ousia* is only there in the creed of Nicaea because of the presence of Constantine himself, wanting to get an agreement for political reasons.

Nicaea of course was the beginning of Arianism in the Church, not the end and for sixty more years the Nicene phrases were almost totally absent from the creeds that were in use, even in clearly non-Arian churches. If for example, the creed or syllabus taught by St Cyril at Jerusalem in 348 AD is examined, none of the crucial Nicene phrases were there but two points are worthy of comment:

1. 'of whose kingdom there will be no end' – this is another example of a phrase that came in to deal with a specific 4th century teaching (that of Marcellus of Ancyra), that the Son's kingdom only lasted while he was incarnate and then he surrendered it to the Father. We have however to be careful

about this: After all Paul did suggest in *1 Corinthians 15.24* what sounds like the opposite of this phrase of the creed: 'After that will come the end, when Christ hands over the kingdom to God the Father, having done away with every sovereignty, authority and power . . . and when everything is subjected to him, then the Son himself will be subject in his turn to the One who subjected all things to him, so that God may be all in all'. Here is another credal phrase where the intention is one thing and the actual words used are another. We recognize that the words used are taken directly from *Luke 1.33*, the Archangel Gabriel's words to Mary, but that does not make the problem disappear.

2.   The third article of the creed on the Holy Spirit is now being amplified by analogy with the west, but not much is being said yet about the nature of the Holy Spirit himself. Some ancient fathers were hesitant about these extra items even though they were ostensibly aspects of the work of the Spirit because they tended to break up the simplicity of the creed as being about God and not about the Church. You could say that we believe in God the Father, we believe in God the Son, we believe in God the Holy Spirit. But you must not say we believe in the church, in the communion of saints: you might believe them but you must not believe in them.

So we came to the final phase in the development of the Nicene Creed when the Council of Constantinople in 381 adopted an expanded version of the creed of Nicaea and this (at the Council of Chalcedon in 451) was claimed as the authentic creed of Christendom, the only ecumenical creed – since the Apostles' creed was only used in the west. So now we have arrived at the text of what we know as the Nicene Creed and the only adjustments to comment on are the phrases about the Spirit, consciously bringing the doctrines about the third Person of the Trinity into line with the other two but also consciously distinguishing the relationship: the Son is 'begotten' of the Father, the Spirit 'proceeds' from the Father. The Spirit is equally Lord with them, equally the giver of life, equally to be worshipped and glorified but distinguished in relationship.

Thus the story of both the Apostles' and the Nicene Creed has been told. But has it? There is still a phrase which we have not mentioned in the Nicene Creed: 'and the Son' – this phrase is not part of this chapter, since it is not part properly of the Nicene Creed but belongs to the use of the creeds and raises many questions which we still have to consider. Are we free to add to the creeds, to change them? Are the creeds static and the last word on all Christian belief? Some of the answers to these questions are given in the history of the church and what English church people have said in the 20th century hence the necessity of the next two chapters. But the story of how these two pre-eminent creeds evolved must be told first since that story itself has provided some hints of the answers to these important questions.

8

The use of the Creeds in the history of the Church

The creeds developed *first* as necessary summary statements of the essence of the Christian faith to serve as the syllabus of baptismal instruction, to lead up to the three questions that were asked of the candidate about to be baptised and confirmed and later 'given back' as the candidate reaffirmed before the congregation in a declaratory form the faith in which he was baptised. We saw that in the east the ancestors of our Nicene creed were used for this purpose and in the west the ancestor of our Apostles' Creed.

Secondly, the creeds were developed in the period after the cessation of persecution when the institution of the church was becoming more important and its visible and communal unity in one faith mattered not only to itself but also to others; and became conciliar affirmations, liable to be added to and adjusted to define more carefully the theological point being made. The 4th century saw the multiplication of creeds and confessions with almost a new one at each Council and it was the future that would determine which were to survive as living expressions of faith and which were to be buried in the archives as records only of what attempts were made at definition that were not finally approved.

The *third* development in the use of creeds that was to have far-reaching implications has now to be noted; it is a strange fact – but not unique in the history of great changes – that it started in an ironic and haphazard way. Those who were defeated at the Council of Chalcedon in 451 – those, that is, who maintained that the Incarnate Christ must have one nature only and regarded the Chalcedonian definition insisting on two natures, as essentially erroneous – marked their rejection of the new definition by protesting openly and

solemnly their allegiance to an older and more respectable –
from their point of view – definition of faith. So they began by
reciting the old Nicene creed in the liturgy of the Mass at
Sancta Sophia in Constantinople and gradually this custom
commended itself to the people even after the original reason
for introducing it was forgotten. The position in the Mass was
after the Offertory and before the Pax, and – as you would
expect in the eastern Orthodox Church, there it has stayed. In
the west, Spain led the way and it was associated with a more
hymnic concept of the creed as a celebration and a rejoicing in
the faith. The creed appeared at the end of the Psalters that
were gradually being published, together with the *Te Deum*
and the *Quicunque Vult*[4] you will recognize that there are
clear credal elements in both these hymns even though the
atmosphere is clearly one of celebration rather than instruction. The Spanish place in the Mass was before the Lord's
Prayer as an immediate preparation for Communion and this
does imply an element of testing the people. There was
probably direct influence on Spain from the east at this point.
Linked to the extension of the use of the creeds in hymnic and
eucharistic assertions of the faith is the pressure that became
intensified to make the creed express the faith as it is now
held.

The great illustration of this is the pressure to add to the
Nicene creed the phrase 'and the son' – the famous *Filioque*
Clause. It was first felt in the west in the 8th century and
became universal in the 11th century AD The teaching of the
early church, expressed in the Nicene creed, was that the three
persons of the Trinity were closely related to each other and
particularly to the Father as the source of everything even in
the Godhead[5]; hence the relationship of the Son to the Father
was described in terms of being *begotten* and the relationship
of the Holy Spirit to the Father in terms of *proceeding*:
obviously this was a search for a word, to avoid on the one
hand the implications of begetting (otherwise you would have
to confess that the Spirit also was the Son of God – or more
likely the daughter of God – if only we had time to follow up
that thought) and so avoiding on the other hand the

implications of creatureliness: the Holy Spirit was not a result of God's creative activity but was one eternal person of the Godhead. So we have the phrase in the extended Nicene creed 'proceeding from the Father who with the Father and the Son is worshipped and glorified'. But this phraseology did not do justice to the clear Biblical language about the Spirit as being Jesus Christ's Spirit – he spoke of giving his Spirit to his disciples and all doctrine about the Spirit was geared to the mediation of the gifts and grace of the Son to the world and to the church just as much, if not actually more than, the Old Testament sense of mediating the life and prophetic inspirations of God himself. So the actual teaching of the early church, in the east as well as in the west, concentrated on the phrase *from the Father, through the Son*. Here we have a formula that unites and, I would think sufficiently, expresses what needs to be said, what we would want to say, about the relation of the Holy Spirit to the other persons of the Trinity.

But it was due to the influence of St Augustine that a more precise and more controversial phrase got hold of the west and began to dominate its thinking on this matter. For St Augustine the Trinity was entirely self-sufficient and interdependent – all that could be said of one Person could be said of the other. So he did not want to preserve the east's notion of the Father as the sole and only source of existence even within the Godhead. He taught explicitly and frequently that the Holy Spirit proceeded both from the Father *and the Son* and this gradually became the generally accepted language in the west.

It is interesting that when this language became particularly valuable to the Western church as a way of asserting the eternal Divinity of the Persons of the Trinity in the face of various teachings that tended to weaken this assertion – such as a resurgence of Arianism and a heresy called Priscillianism both of which were active in Spain in the 5th and 6th centuries AD – then began to move to strengthen the phraseology of the creed itself on this point. At the end of the 6th century in Spain at the council of Toledo in 589, an anathema was pronounced on all who would not confess the double procession of the Spirit, 'Whoever does not believe in the Holy Spirit or does not believe that He proceeds from the Father and the Son, and denies that he is co-eternal and co-equal with the Father and the Son, let him be anathema.'[6] In spite of this it is not absolutely certain that when they affirmed the Nicene creed, it had the vital addition in it. But before long the addition 'and the Son' had been made and it spread through Spain and Gaul to Ireland. From Ireland it spread to Northumbria, and it was through Alcuin and his campaign to unit the west against the east that the phrase became more general in the western creed. For Alcuin and Charlemagne the Nicene creed with this addition was part of the armoury for Western Church Unity; the addition expressed the faith of the Western Church as it had been held for several centuries and to deny it would suggest that you were tainted with Arian principles which the east might well seem to be. There was, so it seemed to Charlemagne, an unanswerable case for accepting this addition to the creed and encouraging its use throughout Europe. After all, so the argument very sensibly went, propounded by St Paulinus of Aquilieia in 794, the creed of the Council of Nicaea itself had been added to by the Fathers of the Council of Constantinople to recognize a further precision in definition of doctrine that had turned out to be necessary, so why not do the same so that the creed of the western church should express the faith of contemporary Christendom?

This position, very significant for our 20th century understanding of creeds and confessions, was connected with another move fostered by Charlemagne. This was to get the creed accepted into the eucharistic liturgy of the church which as we have seen was part of the same tradition that added the *Filioque* to the creed. As part of the Eucharistic liturgy in the place that Alcuin was putting it after the reading of the Gospel, it became a celebration in song of the essence of the Christian faith, responding to and completing that fragment of the Christian faith that had been highlighted in the reading of the gospel. In this way the new usage for the creed was supporting the argument that it ought to reflect the fullness of the Christian faith as it was then believed.

But here Charlemagne was to come up against another tradition and another concept of the purpose of the creeds. Pope Leo III agreed that the doctrine of the double procession was orthodox and was taught in his own church at Rome: but he totally rejected the argument that that meant that the creed should be altered. 'Did you not', asked Charlemagne's messenger 'give him permission to sing that creed in church?' – this means as part of the eucharistic liturgy. 'I did indeed give permission for its singing', retorted Pope Leo III, 'but not for its singing with additions.' Behind this was a twofold opposition. It was not the custom at Rome to use the creed in the liturgy and it was not to be for two more centuries; so there the creed was still primarily a baptismal confession and syllabus of instruction; nor did Rome know the creed with its unauthorized addition and was well aware of the strength of the eastern church's position that one should not alter an ecumenical creed if you had any pretensions whatever to wanting to preserve the authentic agreed teaching of the church and thus its unity. Thus you can see how the objection depended partly on conceptions about what the creeds were for: if as Rome maintained, keeping the ancient traditions, the creeds were baptismal instructions in short summary form, you would expound all the desirable further ramifications and intricacies during the course of your teaching; it was more important to keep the formula short, and above all accurate and ecumenically sound because it expressed the minimum necessary. If as Charlemagne maintained, speaking for a movement that was gaining ground and before which Rome would eventually capitulate, the creed was the solemn liturgical assertion by the church of what she *then* believed – and also, we must admit, you were strong enough and obscurantist enough or convinced enough of your rightness not to worry too much about those who saw things differently, then you would think it more important to guard against false teaching and permit short additions that were clarifications and corrections.

The opposition of Rome to the extra word in the creed (*Filioque*) may have had a second cause: here was a tradition that was growing up in the Western Church not in accordance with Rome's own practice. Whatever sympathy the Pope might feel for the doctrinal point being made, could he be seen to be following the lead of another western custom? Rome was busy fostering the teaching that she was the centre from which authorized change should flow: she could argue that by waiting she was testing the innovation for general acceptance but by too readily and immediately accepting the addition she could only lose face. However this may be, two centuries later Rome capitulated and incorporated the Nicene creed with the *Filioque* addition into the liturgy of the Mass, in the 'Celtic' position (so called because the first written witness to it is in the Stowe Missal) that is after the Gospel.

We have now arrived firmly in the early middle ages; another use of these creeds and confessional statements must be noted: as a personal confession of faith and individual test of orthodoxy. This use obviously began in a very simple way right at the beginning of the development when the candidate for baptism recited or rendered back the outline of the faith in his declaratory baptismal creed. But with the gradual expansion and solidification of the dogmatic structure of the faith there came a confidence that these summaries of it expressed the essence of eternal truth and not only needed to be assented to totally with all one's mind but also repeated continually and learnt by heart. This particularly applied to the clergy but the following two quotations show that it by no means only applied to them. In one of his sermons St Augustine said:

> When you rise, when you lie down to sleep, repeat your creed, repeat it to God . . . Do not say, 'I said it yesterday, I have said it today, I say it every day. I can remember it very well.' Rehearse your faith, look into yourself: let your creed be as a mirror to you. Look at yourself in it to see whether you believe all you say you believe, and rejoice in your faith each day.[8]

And St Paulinus of Aquileia, the contemporary of Alcuin said,

The Creed and the Paternoster must be known by heart by every Christian, every age, sex and condition, men and women, the servants and the freedmen, the boys and the married men as well as unmarried girls; for without this blessing no one will be able to obtain his share in the kingdom of heaven.

Better known perhaps are the uncompromising words of the so-called Athanasian Creed at the end, 'This is the Catholic Faith: unless a man believes it faithfully and steadfastly, he will not be able to be saved.' There are two aspects to this: one is the individual profession of faith: 'I believe this.' The other, equally important but one we are inclined to forget, is the blessing that the recitation of the faith can give to you. This is noticeable in the Augustine sermon where the 'rejoicing in your faith' is mentioned and in the Paulinus quotation where he speaks of the creeds as a blessing. This last point links up with the use of the creeds as hymns and canticles; and it is also implied in the further development of the inclusions of the western church. The *Te Deum* is known as a part of the offices from the 6th century and the so-called Athanasian and Apostles' Creeds also gain ground in the offices in the 7th–9th centuries AD.

Before we come to the Reformation there is one other point to be made. The absolute confidence of our forefathers in the faith from Patristic times to, at any rate, the 18th century that God's exact revelation of himself and his truth was known in the words of Scripture and in the approved summaries of Scriptural truth that we call creeds, was not totally monolythic and unchallenged. I mentioned in the last chapter the reluctance of the orthodox bishops of Nicaea to accept the *Homoousion* because it seemed to go beyond what could be unequivocally asserted on the basis of Scripture. Hilary of Poitiers in the decades following Nicea, himself a defender of the Nicene faith, has these fine words to say:

Faithful souls would be contented with the word of God which tells us 'Go teach all nations, baptising them in the name of the Father, the Son and the Holy Spirit' – but we are drawn by the faults of our heretical opponents to do things unlawful, to scale heights inaccessible, to speak out what is unspeakable, to presume where we ought not. Whereas it is by the faith alone that we should worship the Father and reverence the Son and be filled with the Spirit, we are now obliged to strain our weak human language in the utterance of things beyond its scope.[9]

St Augustine makes a similar point in his work on the Trinity; he confesses that when he is asked by people what 'persons' mean in the Trinitarian formula, he has to admit that human speech is embarrassed by the great poverty of language:

However we say three Persons, not because that expresses just what we want to say, but because we must say something.[10]

These great minds are speaking here precisely about the subject matter of councils and creeds and they provide a necessary anchor against the enthusiastic voices that see both the words of Scripture and also the words of the creeds as direct, permanent expressions of the truth, proceeding straight from God.

The western church was convulsed by further disagreements and schisms, and ennobled by further councils and confessions in the era we call that of the Reformation. Yet in one respect nothing much was changed: the controversies were not about the matters debated in patristic times and therefore the new parts of the fragmented church were able to continue the assertion, which had been common in the west since the 13th century, that they stood by the so-called three ecumenical creeds, the Apostles', the Nicene, and the Athanasian creeds. (However there is an irony in this since none of the creeds is completely and absolutely ecumenical. The Apostles' Creed is not used in the Eastern church, the Athanasian Creed had a very chequered history in the east of recognition and rejection but had never been regarded as an ecumenical creed and of course the Nicene Creed has its text in dispute). The attitude to the words of the creed remained much the same as during the middle ages and that great

English expositor of creeds, Bishop Pearson, expresses the almost universal view of his time, when he defines belief in a rather intellectual way as 'assent to that which is credible'[11] when the assent in question is not obvious or tangible or logical but is founded upon acceptance of the testimony given to it.

> To believe therefore is to assent to the whole and every part of it, as to a certain and infallible truth revealed by God and delivered unto us in the writings of the blessed Apostles and Prophets immediately inspired, moved and acted by God, out of whose writings this brief sum of necessary points of Faith was first collected.

The assent to every 'article and particle' of the creed is founded upon the assertion that because it is a summary of what the Apostles said, it has the direct authority of God himself. The reasons for taking this absolute attitude to the contents of the creed do vary with different writers; some lean heavily on the legend that the twelve apostles actually wrote the Apostles' Creed, others on the views either that the Church, the Bishops or the Pope has authorized the creeds, but the attitude is almost universal.

Jeremy Taylor, however, may be taken as striking a rather different note: he had his doubts about the Athanasian Creed and in particular the damnatory clauses:

> they are extrinsical and accidental to the articles and might as well have been spared. And indeed to me, it seems very hard to put uncharitableness into the creed, and so to make it become an article of faith.[12]

He goes on to doubt whether this creed was ever meant to be a creed imposed on others, he thought it was rather a declaration of the faith of a particular individual. Here we see the exercise of reason in the context of scholarship and not an acceptance of the creeds merely on the assumption that they bear the stamp of God's own authority.

But at the Reformation of course the creeds were no longer the points at issue: a general unity throughout the Reformation was maintained on the Trinity and the Person of Christ and the focus shifted to other matters where all was changed. Adherence to Christian truth now required more detailed assent to another set of recent confessional statements; for the Lutherans it was the Augsburg Confession of 1530; for the Calvinists both Calvin's own Institutes and the Heidelburg Catechism of 1563; for the Roman Catholics it was the creed of the Council of Trent of 1564 and the Anglicans depended primarily on the 39 Articles of 1571. Now these confessions were not in any way equally regarded nor did they play exactly the same role in each of the different communions; but from now on a confession of the faith had to be made in the context of one or other of these various Reformation statements, – the three ecumenical creeds themselves were not enough on their own because they no longer now denoted any recognizable Christian fellowship. Yet it is a noticeable fact that on the whole, and of course this is a generalization, the assent to these further and more recent formulae was required only from the clergy and ministers and the simpler and more traditional confessions were all that was required from the laity. I take most of my examples in the succeeding paragraphs mainly from the Church of England.

Subscription to some of the 39 Articles required by Parliament in 1571 for ordination candidates and those presented to benefices and to all of the 39 Articles in the Canon of 1604 is stated in the following words, 'I do willingly and *ex animo* subscribe to these three articles above mentioned (i.e. Royal Supremacy, The Book of Common Prayer and the 39 Articles) and to all things that are contained in them.' Subscription was required also for a time for those entering the universities of Oxford and Cambridge, for judges in ecclesiastical courts and, in recent times, for Deaconesses and Readers. There were those who argued that subscription to the Articles meant total committal to every phrase and that the comprehensiveness of the Church of England was shown by the imprecision of the Articles when compared to some of the other Reformation confessions.[13] Others argued that since the Articles were Articles of Peace all that was required was an undertaking not to contradict them in public. The fact that assent to the articles was not required of laymen has been claimed to point to a significant difference between these and the Catholic creeds. Admittedly both are statements of faith but the creeds are for all and are permanent, the confessions are for ministers and are temporary, created by the failure of the church to agree. Bicknell sums up his arguing of this point thus: 'Creeds belong to the life of the church and Articles to its life in a sinful world.'[14] The strength of this argument for a distinction in quality is clear: a distinction in usage is clear: but a distinction in kind is harder to establish. Similar professions of faith were required in other communions at this time since many justifications of confessional writings, the ancient creeds as well as the Reformation confessions, are based on them as being expositions of Scripture: they bear no other authority than their claim to present the essence of what God reveals in His Holy Word.

The 17th century was a period of dogmatism and conviction about details: the confessional boundaries were drawn up, fought over and died for in a way that we find, I think, very difficult to sympathize with, even though we are seeing a resurgence of this kind of thing in our own time. But the 18th century introduced a rationalism that spread its influence throughout Europe. Creeds began to get a bad name in some quarters and moves were made to release clergy from the burden of subscription to the 39 Articles. It took into the next century for these moves to have much fruition, but by then a new spirit was on the way. Huxley said, 'Science commits suicide the moment it accepts a creed'[15] and Christian defenders of creeds and confessions admitted that they sometimes 'powerfully tended to bias men's minds with reference to the single-eyed investigation of truth'. On this point it is quite truly said by opponents of Confessions that they operate by disposing a man to avoid frank and perfectly sincere investigation when doubts or questions arise which, as he foresees, might bring him into collision with the confessional teaching. He is tempted to form a habit of undue deference to the human document, to the consent which it expresses and the antiquity which invests it. This is the voice of the 19th century and a change in the form of subscription to the 39 Articles in 1865 is only one of the signs of a new attitude to the past.

But now we are at the roots of our present debates; open rejection of parts of the 16th century statements of faith have been a feature of church life for more than 150 years and this century has seen the questioning of phrases in the ecumenical creeds not only by freethinkers and scholars but by devout worshippers, clergy and bishops: but the 20th century is the subject of the next chapter and I will bring this survey of many hundred years to a close with one general remark.

As a very new student of theology I remember going to my first set of doctrine lectures and hearing Professor H.E.W. Turner speaking about *lex orandi, lex credeni*. It took me a long time to know the implications of what he was saying and the importance of this tag. Succinctly it means 'worship first, then doctrine', or more elaborately the church worships and through its worship it learns the words to express what it believes. Creeds, confessions, summaries of belief are essential in a world that thinks, worships and communicates through words; but that does not mean that everything changes because the words must ring true to experience and the experience is corporate, historic and continuous. You may feel sad at the verbal differences that there have been between Christians; but if you think of the loyalty, devotion, even ecstasy for God in Christ that has led to the struggles for the right words to express it you cannot but rejoice at it and be glad to be of their company and in their company. Learn to love every sermon, every utterance in a discussion group, even every lecture, because it is only a more personal, more temporary version of a creed or confession. See it was someone trying to be accurate and interesting and genuine about the Faith. Your mind will rightly want to say, 'Yes, but' . . . but let your heart join in with the hymn-like aspect of what is happening: someone speaking out of worship and towards worship.

9

Saying the Creeds Today

The historical context of this chapter (for even what was said or written yesterday is history) is the last hundred years: this is not so far back as you might think for many of the events of the last few years are in some aspects a strange re-run of the early decades of this century. I wish to start with a few sentences from Owen Chadwick's biography of Hensley Henson about his hesitation over going forward to ordination:

> Men of 1886–7, thinking of ordination, had a special reason for hesitation. Could they believe the faith which the Church of England professed? The eighties were the full tide of battle between science and religion, and of anxious argument over the truth of the Bible. If a man took orders was he pretending that he believed in Adam and Eve, or Noah's flood? Must he believe from the depths of his heart that Jesus was born of a Virgin Mother, or could he honestly take orders if his judgement did not know? An Anglican clergyman must subscribe to the 39 Articles of Religion, drafted in the reign of Queen Elizabeth I as the Anglican statement of a Protestant creed. To subscribe these was not difficult, because an Act of 1865 made assent to the 39 Articles 'general' and did not commit the future clergyman to every detail or every proposition ... But could he believe enough to be honestly ordained?[16]

Chadwick describes this as a live issue a hundred years ago and the evidence is of course in the famous names and causes that brought these issues before the attention of the European public at the end of the last century and the beginning of this,

such as the gradual effects of the Biblical work of Schleier-
macher, Strauss, Harnack and Schweitzer; the controversies
surrounding F.D. Maurice and the authors of *Essays and
Reviews*, the appointment of Frederick Temple as Bishop of
Exeter in 1981, the controversies surrounding Professor
Hastings Rashdall and the authors of *Foundations* and the
continental modernists like Renan and Loisy. All this was
focused in the perplexities of many Christian minds and in the
hesitations of many clergy at their ordination of whom the
most famous were Hensley Henson and William Temple.

It is interesting that in England the point of attack chosen
by those wanting to defend the hitherto accepted orthodoxies,
(men such as Charles Gore and Frank Weston) was the
honesty of affirming the creeds and subscribing to the Articles
if you thought like that. Roger Lloyd in his rather oddly
named book *The Church of England in the 20th century*[17]
which tells the story from 1900–1939, points out that on the
continent, and in the Roman Catholic Church generally, the
cry of heresy was raised and the whole might of the judicial
system was brought in to condemn, excommunicate and
silence until these voices have begun to break through again in
the Roman Catholic Church in our own time. But in England
it was different:

> persecution for matters of individual beliefs is quite
> alien to the English temperament and the Church of
> England had been so built through the centuries as to
> make every method of regimenting and proscribing
> freely uttered opinion almost impossible to apply . . .
> Besides all this, there is always the reaction of the
> general public as well as the mass of church people to
> bear in mind. It is poor tactics to brand and punish a
> man as a heretic when the very fact and title would
> automatically make him a hero, and the prosecuting
> bishop a bigot and a tyrant to nine tenths of the people.
> But inconsistency was a charge everyone understood
> and set at its proper value. Thus in England it was
> plainly the right point on which to join issue. It meant in

practice that the excommunication and proscriptions which were so marked a feature of the struggle abroad were kept out of the story of the conflict in England. Thus in the end that which was creative in Anglican modernism was able to find its place within and make its contribution to, Anglican doctrine.

It is this very charge of inconsistency of course that raises in acute form the subject matter of these enquiries: what are the creeds and credal formularies for? Do we use them rightly? Should they be altered? Must we require belief in them from our clergy and bishops if not from laypeople? The cynic might say that the controversies of the early part of this century highlighted two uses of the creeds that I have not hitherto mentioned: one, as an obstacle to be surmounted or evaded before the Lord's work can be done, and second, as a club with which to hammer those with whom one disagrees; but let us now take a more serious look at some of the major incidents at the beginning of our century.

Charles Gore, Bishop of Worcester, appealed to the new Archbishop of Canterbury, Randall Davidson in 1903 to agree to a declaration that the bishops would not connive at men being ordained who did not believe in the Articles of the Creed – particularly the Virgin Birth.[18] By believing the Virgin Birth, Gore did not mean believing that Jesus was the incarnate Son of God, both God and man with a human nature like ours: what he meant was that Jesus' birth of a Virgin Mother was an historical fact that secured and guaranteed the Incarnation. To issue such a declaration would be virtually 'an addition to our formularies' said the cautious Davidson, and the Dean of Westminster, Armitage Robinson stopped the whole process when he wrote:

> If the Bishops were asked to declare that the Incarnation is a cardinal doctrine of the faith, such a statement would be superfluous, but it would be true. But to say that the historical fact of the Virgin Birth is a cardinal doctrine of the faith is to use language which no Synod of Bishops so far as I am aware has ever ventured to use.

It is to confuse the Incarnation with the special mode of the Incarnation in a way for which Christian theology offers no precedent.

Further incidents occurred around R.J.Campbell of the City Temple and Professor William Sanday of Oxford: things got even fiercer with the Kikuyu incident in 1913, when Frank Weston, Bishop of Zanzibar denounced his brother bishops for heresy and Gore on one side, and Hensley Henson, now Dean of Durham on the other, took up the cudgels and Davidson tried to keep an even keel.[19] It would be a misrepresentation of the situation to say that this was simply a confrontation between obscurantism and tolerance. Bishop Weston was in a missionary situation concerned with simple believers and simple enemies and it was out of that situation that he spoke:

> I do not hesitate to say that a Church which has two views in its highest ranks about the trustworthiness of the Bible, the authority of the Church, and the infallibility of the Christ has surrendered its chance of winning the Moslem; for his dependence upon his Book, his tradition and his Prophet will not be broken by a debating society, but by the living, speaking Church of the Infallible Word Incarnate.

This raises a very important point. There is a genuine cry here that is echoed in many of those voices that have come after: but inasmuch as the cry asks for simple verbal and historical certainties in areas where, in my opinion, the nature of the events and the limitations of our knowledge and language will not allow such certainty, that cry must go always unanswered – indeed where it is satisfied a misrepresentation of the faith is being offered. Where that cry ought to be answered, and where it is asking for something it ought to have, is in its appeal against giving the impression that the Church has 'two views' and is content to leave it like that: there is a mean between that and the one voice which is so monolythic and uniform that all nuances and openness to the future is eradicated. I doubt whether the English churches have really seen the danger in the situation where clergy are trained in one view at their studies and encouraged to behave in church as if everything was still as it was. Perhaps this is one of the reasons why we are now having this re-run of the issues: our negligences are catching up with us, focused most monstrously in that phenomenon which all teachers of theology know, the student who adopts one view in his academic work because that is what is wanted there and a totally different one in his church because that is what he thinks is wanted there.

In 1917 there occurred another event that caused much excitement and has both startling parallels and clear differences from recent events in the Church of England. A great defender of the rights of clergymen to be sceptical about the Virgin Birth and the physical resurrection, and one who by no means concurred with the notion that if you doubted these things you should keep quiet about your doubts, namely Dr Hensley Henson, Dean of Durham, was nominated as Bishop of Hereford. If I said that 'all hell was let loose' you might think I was being partisan! But at any rate there was deep disquiet from wide sections of the English churches up to and including many of the bishops: and the one who bore the brunt was the consecrator, Randall Davidson, just over half way through his 25 years as Archbishop of Canterbury. A thirty page chapter in Bell's biography records the *furore*;[20] the outcome was a desperate appeal from Davidson to Henson to be allowed to publish some kind of statement of faith; Henson felt that his published works were his statement and he could not add to what was said there: Davidson felt that the published works were the cause of the trouble and something else was necessary. After very great pressure from Davidson, Henson agreed to a statement that contained the following words:

> I repeat and accept the words of the Creed *ex animo*. I use them without any sense of incongruity, and with no desire to change them ... When in the Creed I affirm, as I readily do, that traditional belief of the Church in

the birth of Jesus Christ without a human father, I am bound to add that the belief in the Incarnation may be consistent now, as it was consistent in Apostolic days, with other notions or explanations of the mode of what happened therein. I have never seen any satisfying alternative to the dogma of the Virgin Birth.

Davidson declared he could proceed with the consecration, Gore withdrew his objections somewhat grudgingly and Henson threw himself into being a good bishop, first at Hereford for a short time and then for ten years as Bishop of Durham. Randall Davidson recorded the time of this controversy as being 'the most anxious and harrowing weeks in the whole of my life'.

Gradually, however, both Henson and the climate in England was changing. The three parties were becoming less significant and less vocal. The Modernism of the early decades of the century was fading away, the Evangelicals were settling into a period of petulant obscurantism and the Anglo-Catholics, sensing a practical victory in the Church, began to feel that they did not need intellectuals to help them with any more argument. The mood of English Christianity was moving fast towards the new Biblical theology, social Christianity and ecumenicism. Things were more stable, less frantic, more reasonable, hopeful and exciting. Moves began to be made to help the churches assimilate into their corporate thinking the tensions between the old orthodoxies and the not-so-new attitudes and emphases that were fast becoming the new orthodoxy and to assimilate the results of the contacts over the denominational boundaries. The most important purely Anglican expression of this was the Report of the Commission on Christian Doctrine appointed by the Archbishops of Canterbury and York in 1922 that saw the light of day sixteen years later in 1938, a document that is only in the last decade or so really receiving its proper evaluation. A lot can happen in sixteen years and the second world war in effect killed this document as a publication.

There is an intriguing appended note in this Report on the

application to the Creeds of the Conception of Symbolic Truth;[21] it recognizes that the language of the creeds and articles is symbolic in the sense that they carry other meanings than only the historical and metaphysical and recognizes even more pertinently that some of the credal phrases may be symbolic in the sense that they 'have value as pictorial expressions of spiritual truths, even though the supposed facts themselves did not actually happen'. 'It is not therefore of necessity illegitimate to accept and affirm particular clauses of the creeds while understanding them in this symbolic sense.' I suppose that the language about the Ascension is the most obvious example of this, one which I imagine hardly anyone in today's church would dispute is symbolic in precisely this sense: even though the early Church thought that Jesus went up physically into heaven it is not the main point of the phrase in the creed and we can believe the lordship of Christ and the cessation of his resurrection appearances without needing to believe that he actually went upwards in the sky. The fact that we all accept this now is a measure of the extent to which the church has corporately moved during the 20th century. The 1938 note goes on to say that nevertheless the facts underlying the Gospel story were such as to justify the Gospel itself and that the 'broad tradition' about Jesus must be accepted as historical. This emphasis on 'general assent' is carried on in the next note on Assent: general assent to the creeds and formularies is required but not detailed assent to every phrase or proposition.[22] And it goes on in a section agreed by the whole Commission: 'A member of the Church should not be held to be involved in dishonesty from the tradition of the Church, he has assented to formularies or *makes use of the Church's liturgical language in public worship*.' The above considerations apply to the authorized teachers as well as to all other members of the Church; but the position of the authorized teacher is distinctive, and the Church has a right to satisfy itself and those who teach in its name *adequately represent and express its mind*.

The two phrases deserve pondering over as much for what they do not say as for what they do: 'Makes use of . . . etc:

here is the clear recognition that there is a proper dichotomy between individual and corporate faith and that the extensive use that the Anglican church makes of the creeds in its liturgy – more than any other church – places the creeds – in this use of them as affirmations of personal faith when saying the creeds in the church service, but affirming his membership of a body for whom this is an ancient summary of its faith. The other phrase worth a comment is 'adequately represent . . . etc.' The 'authorized teachers' here are not only bishops but other clergy, deaconnesses and readers, all in fact who were called to assent to the 39 Articles: there is both a permission and a requirement here; it is the mind of the church that must be fairly represented and where the mind is indecisive or changing no one can be blamed for not being precise: but an authorized teacher must also be honest, not only to himself, but also to the church that authorizes him; people must know when he is expressing an opinion purely personal for they rightly assume that on public teaching or preaching Christianity is not in fact communicating an existing body of knowledge: it cannot be equated with an authorized law teacher and the 'mind of the church' is a very fluid idea altogether, unless you keep committing it to paper through some authorized body which the Anglican church is reluctant to do.

The next point flows directly from this. In the post war years it was increasingly felt that the 39 Articles of Religion no longer fairly represented 'the mind of the church' and that even the general form of assent to them should be modified or abandoned. Their historic importance was universally acknowledged; they defined the position of the English church at the time of the Reformation as distinct from both the Tridentine Roman Catholics on the one hand and the Presbyterians on the other: that is where we stood and nothing can alter that; and, most Anglicans would say, given the same situation – which is of course impossible but it is a nice point – we would stand in the same place; in that sense the Articles are not just historic documents but they do state a position in relation to the other two positions. Archbishop

Garbett used to explain to his ordinands that subscription is an expression of loyalty to the faith of the Church and that no man could honestly subscribe if he rejected belief in the supernatural or held that either Romans or Puritans were right in their controversies with our Church. The bit about the 'supernatural' is interesting, there is a personal interpretation here which seems to have no standing in either the Creeds or the Articles although it is clearly intended to be a broad acceptance that the events of the Creed could have happened. But the issue of the contemporary status of the Articles was big enough in the 60's for several books and a special report from the Archbishops' Commission on Christian doctrine which was published in 1968.[23]

Before going on to what happened as a result of this, there are several interesting items from the preliminary discussion.[24] There is a difference of opinion about whether the 39 Articles, and other denominational formulae like the Augsburg Confession or the Council of Trent decisions, are fundamentally in the same category as the ancient creeds or not. Professor G.Lampe argues that they are not; they are not so ancient, they are not recognized universally by Christians, they do not form part of acts of worship. This means that they are much more tied to their original purpose, and limited in the relevance they have for a 20th century church; the creeds on the other hand hold their place now as markers and summaries of the faith in a way which all churches hold in common. They do not on most matters go into much interpretative detail. A good example of this last difference is the treatment of the Resurrection and the Ascension. The two creeds both say: 'On the third day He rose again, He ascended into heaven' (Apostles); 'On the third day He rose again in accordance with the Scriptures; He ascended into heaven and is seated at the right hand of the Father' (Nicene). The Articles say; 'Christ did truly rise again from death, and took again his body, with flesh, bones and all things pertaining to Man's nature; wherewith He ascended into Heaven, and there sitteth'. The emphasis is on the physical body in both rising and ascending because it is Man's nature that must be exalted.

The creed allows us to affirm the lordship of Christ with God and his triumph over death and his redemption of human nature; but the Article forces an interpretation of that which cannot be the only possible one in the 20th century. So Lampe argued that the Articles should be put on the shelf labelled 'history' and not referred to as standards of doctrine; but that the creeds, though equally historic, still had a vital part to play in the worship and unity of the Church.

Dr J.Packer argued for the retention of the Articles but subsumed both them and the creeds to the higher authority of Scriptures, which for him are the sole source of God's revelation; the only authority that formularies can claim is as an accurate summary of Scripture:

> Even the creeds remain human: we never dare treat them as intrinsically inerrant, no matter how many millions of people endorse them. The creeds and the Articles alike come to us as venerable commentaries on, and primary expositions of Holy Scripture: no more, no less. Because they are no more than that none of us is free from the responsibility of testing and measuring them by the Scriptures which they seek to expound. But because they are no less than this, and because the church of which we are part has ventured to commit itself to them as sound expositions, none of us is free to neglect or ignore or slight them.

In those two contributions we have the neo-liberal and the neo-evangelical emphasis. We are not back in the early years of the 20th century because the resurgence of both liberalism and evangelicalism in the 1970s and 80s is a different thing from the old; they have both absorbed the biblical criticism and the biblical theology movement and are able to understand each other better. A new formula of assent for the authorized teachers of the Church of England followed in the 1960s and as this is now the current statement of the status of both creeds and Articles it deserves to be quoted. There is a Preface to the declaration which, after stating that the Church of England is part of the Catholic Church goes on:

> It professes the faith uniquely revealed in the Holy Scriptures and set forth in the Catholic creeds, which faith the church is called upon to proclaim afresh in each generation. Led by the Holy Spirit, it has borne witness to Christian truth in its historic formularies, the 39 Articles of Religion, the Book of Common Prayer and the Orderings of Bishops, Priests and Deacons . . . will you affirm your loyalty to this inheritance of faith as your inspiration and guidance . . .

and the actual declaration is;

> I declare my belief in the faith which is revealed in the Holy Scriptures and set forth in the Catholic Creeds and to which the historic formularies of the Church of England bear witness.

These phrases show that things have moved since 1917: the faith is revealed in the Scriptures, set forth in the creeds but it must be proclaimed afresh in each generation. The Church of England has borne witness to this faith in its historic formularies – now wider than just the 39 Articles – and the Anglican must be inspired and guided by this historic inheritance in the present tasks of teaching and caring. Nevertheless these formularies are clearly announced to be the standard of declared doctrine in the modern Church of England and, as the 1981 Doctrine Commission Report declares; 'If this causes problems, they are problems that the church has declared that she intends to live with.'[25]

Much time has been spent on the issue of the creeds and formularies as standards of doctrine and the senses in which 'official' Anglicans have been required to assent to them. But this, I think is worth while because it has focused many of the issues that exist in no less serious a way, for members of other denominations and congregations faced with the Apostles' or the Nicene creeds at almost every service they attend. This excessive use of the creeds in the Anglican tradition means that the issue is at its sharpest here both for clergy and laypeople. The great disadvantage of this extensive use is that nowadays not all the congregation are baptized Christians who can be expected to be able to cope with saying the creeds; the personal baptismal confession of faith comes very oddly at a Civic Mattins or at a Harvest Evensong; I fear it does much to encourage the notion that everyone irrespective of beliefs is a Christian and that the details of belief need not be taken seriously. Perhaps our ecumenical contacts will help persuade us away from this 'creeds with everything' approach. The corporate creed, 'We believe', at the Eucharist is another matter; here we are rejoicing in the completeness of our faith in the credal summary which is nearly universal throughout the Christian church.[26] We are completing our own inadequacies of faith and understanding in the great sea of faith and devotion which is the universal Christian tradition. Recently a book was published entitled; 'Won't you join the Dance?' by Angela Tilby;[27] it is not a ballroom or disco manual but about the creeds; the idea of the title is a romantic but attractive one. The creeds, she writes, are –

> living symbols which reach out to and reflect back, the mystery of the universe. That mystery is here seen is a dance; a loving, round, gracious dance with very simple steps, lots of room for improvisation, lots of changes within a constant evolving pattern.

I am not sure that the text of the book carries through with this idea but here is a very different way of participating in the creeds from screwing oneself up to believe every word; 'The heart of the Christian faith', she writes,

> is not individual believing but a shared quest, a communal pilgrimage, a dance. Our guest is shared with Christians of the past. To understand the faith we need to take that past seriously, not to deny it or repress it, but to use it as a creative memory, a springboard to hope.

She is here pinpointing something that is perhaps the fundamental contribution of the late 20th century to the understanding of dogmatic formulae. If the 19th century convinced the Church that doctrine does indeed develop and if the early 20th century convinced the Church that much of the language of dogma is symbolic in character then perhaps the late 20th century will alert the Church to the proper function of the past, which is to push us towards the future. Probably the most widely used textbook in recent decades in England has been John Macquarrie's *Principles of Christian Theology*:[28] he writes that dogma and dogmatic formulae have three distinguishing marks: a basis in the revelation: it is proposed by the church as expressing the mind of the community on a particular issue and it has a conceptual and propositional form often using philosophical terminology. Because of this third mark, it cannot be repeated unaltered today, but today's theologian cannot reject it either; he must exercise what Macquarrie calls 'repetitive thinking' which he describes as

> going in to some experience that has been handed down in such a way that it is, so to speak, brought into the present and its insights and possibilities made alive again. When it is remembered that dogmas were usually formulated to exclude particular errors, so that they are frequently more explicit in what they rule out than in what they affirm, it will be understood that the formulation of a dogma does not mean that some final point has been reached and that future generations are excused from reflecting any more on the matter.

And he quotes Karl Rahner:

> The clearest formulations, the most sanctified formulae, the classic condensations of the centuries – long work of the Church in prayer, reflection and struggle concerning God's mysteries: all these derive their life from the fact that they are not the end but the beginning, not goals, but means, truths which open the way to the even greater Truth.

When we say or sing the creeds today then, we are freely, joyfully and without qualification affirming for ourselves, individually and corporately, that faith in God, in Jesus and in the Holy Spirit that has moved and inspired and made whole our fellow Christians for nearly two thousand years. We know that we are using ancient words, some of which reflect ancient controversies and ways of thinking that are not ours today. We are not committing ourselves to all the meanings of all the words, or to all the meanings intended by those who framed the creeds – that would imply a static church, fixed into the past. But we do by affirming them *in toto*, recognize that our faith, not our interpretation or explanation of it, must be the same as theirs: so we make use of their words, freely, joyfully and without qualification and then get on with the task, as they did, of finding and using our own words for praying and evangelizing in the 20th century.

The Evolution of the Creeds

CREEDS OF THE EASTERN CHURCH THAT MAKE UP
THE 'NICENE' CREED

We believe in one God the Father, the Almighty,
maker of heaven and earth, **of all that is seen and unseen**

We believe **in one Lord Jesus Christ**
the only begotten Son of God, **eternally begotten of the Father**

God from God, Light from Light,
TRUE GOD FROM TRUE GOD   begotten
NOT MADE, OF ONE BEING WITH THE FATHER
Through him all things were made

FOR US MEN AND
for our salvation he came down from heaven;
by the power of the Holy Spirit **he became incarnate**

of the Virgin Mary and was made man
For our sake he was crucified under Pontius Pilate

he suffered death and was buried

On the third day he rose again in accordance with the

Scriptures
he ascended into heaven

and is seated at the right hand of the Father

He will come again in glory to judge the living and the dead

and his kingdom will have no end

We believe in the Holy Spirit

the Lord, the Giver of Life, who proceeds from the Father*
With the Father and the Son he is worshipped and glorified.
He has spoken through the Prophets

We believe <u>in one holy Catholic</u> and Apostolic <u>Church</u>
<u>We acknowledge one baptism for the forgiveness of sins</u>
<u>We look for the resurrection of the dead</u>
<u>and the life of the world to come.</u>

* At this point much later Western tradition adds the phrase "and the Son"

KEY

The creed printed in heavy type is the baptismal creed of Caesarea (early 4th Century AD or earlier) quoted by its bishop Eusebius at Nicaea, 325 AD

The phrases in CAPITAL LETTERS are those added at the Council of Nicaea, 325 AD, to make the original synodal creed of Nicaea

<u>The creed underlined</u> is the baptismal creed of Jerusalem as quoted by St Cyril (mid 4th century AD)

The complete text is the traditional "Nicene" creed as established at the Councils of Constantinople (381 AD) and Chalcedon (451 AD)

CREEDS FROM THE WESTERN CHURCH WHICH LATER BECAME THE APOSTLES' CREED

<u>Do you</u>   **believe in God the Father Almighty**
  I

CREATOR OF HEAVEN AND EARTH
<u>Do you believe</u> **in Christ Jesus his only <u>Son</u> our Lord**
    and

HE WAS CONCEIVED   <u>by the Holy Spirit</u>
born from the Virgin Mary
SUFFERED <u>under Pontius Pilate</u>
<u>was crucified</u> died **and was buried**
HE DESCENDED TO THE DEAD
<u>On the third day he rose again, he ascended into heaven</u>
<u>and is seated at the right hand of the Father</u>
<u>he will come to judge the living and the dead</u>

<u>Do you believe</u> **in the Holy Spirit**
    and

the Holy CATHOLIC **church**
THE COMMUNION OF SAINTS
The forgiveness of sins
the resurrection of the flesh
AND THE LIFE EVERLASTING

KEY

<u>Underlined:</u>	the baptismal questions in Hippolytus' *Apostolic Tradition*, 4th century AD
Heavy type:	the baptismal creed of Rome from Rufinus, early 5th century AD
CAPITAL LETTERS:	the phrases added in subsequent centuries to make the traditional text of the Apostles' Creed

Notes

Part 1

1. e.g. Col. 1.16.
2. A.T.Hanson *Studies in Paul's Technique & Theology* 1974, p.90.
3. Jn. 1.45, 6.42.
4. cf Jn. 9.29.
5. Jn. 1.13.
6. Matthew 13.55 and Mark 6.3 where it is in the oldest source although perhaps the original was 'the carpenter, the Son of Mary').
7. Geza Vermes *Jesus the Jew* 1973, p.218–20.
8. Lk. 1.35.
9. A.R.C.Leaney *A Commentary on the Gospel according to St Luke* 1958, p.23.
10. H.Hendrickx *The Infancy Narratives* 1984, p.35.
11. Aquinas quoting Aristotle, J.A.T.Robinson *Human Face of God* 1972, p.50.
12. Emil Brunner *The Mediator* 1934, pp.324–5.
13. J.A.T.Robinson *The Human Face of God* pp.44–48.
14. W.Pannenberg *Jesus God and Man* 1968, p.150.
15. *The Nature of Christian Belief* (Church House Publishing, London 1986, p.33). If one assents to that view therefore one can say the words as affirming not only the Church's 'intention' but also its actual 'mode of expression'.
16. p.326.
17. Markan: 19; M.3; Lk.5: Q.1.
18. Jn. 20.30f.
19. J.Macquarrie, *Principles of Christian Theology*, 1977, p.252.
20. E.Schillebeeckx *Jesus* 1979, pp.180–200.
21. Lk. 5.1–11.
22. Jn. 21.4–8.
23. Lk. 5.8.
24. J.Marsh Pelican Commentary on John, 1968, p.663.
25. E.Hoskyns & F.N.Davey *The Fourth Gospel* 1940, p.553.
26. Mk. 4.35–41. Mt. 8.23–27. Lk.8.22–25.

27. Mk. 6.30–44 8.1–9. Mt. 14.13–21 15.32–38. Lk. 9.10–17. Jn. 6.1–15.
28. Ex. 16 & Num. 11.
29. 1 Kings 17.1–15. 2 Kings 4.38–44.
30. Mk. 6.47–53. Mt. 14.24–33. Jn. 6.16–21.
31. C.F.D.Moule *The Gospel according to Mark* Cambridge Commentaries 1965, p.52.
32. Mt. 17.24–27.
33. Schillebeeckx *Jesus*, p.189.
34. Mk. 11.12–14, 20–22. Mt. 21.18–21.
35. R.V.G.Tasker *Matthew* Tyndale 1961, p.201.
36. Jn. 2.1–11.
37. E.Hoskyns & F.N.Davey *The Fourth Gospel* 1940, p.192.
38. Phema Perkins *Resurrection* 1985, p.48.
39. cf J.A.T.Robinson *The Most Primitive Christology of all* in *Twelve New Testament Essays* 1962, p.140ff.
40. Ulrich Wilckens *Resurrection* 1977, p.20.
41. X.Loen-Dufour S.G. *Resurrection & the Message of Easter* 1974, p.24.
42. T.Harrison *The Durham Phenomenon* 1985, p.22.
43. cf J.A.T.Robinson *The Body* 1952, p.58.
44. Willi Marxsen *The Resurrection of Jesus of Nazareth* 1970, pp.150–2.

Part 2

1. A useful bibliography on Christology is to be found in S.M.Ogden *The Point of Christology* 1982: the following are recommended as being among those easier to read: D.M.Bailiie, *God was in Christ* 1948; J.A.T.Robinson *Honest to God* 1963, chap 4; E.G.Jay *Son of Man–Son of God* 1965; J.Knox, *The Humanity & Divinity of Christ* 1967; ed.N.Pittenger, *Christ for us today* 1968; J.A.Baker, *The Foolishness of God* 1970 Part 2; J.A.T.Robinson, *The Human Face of God* 1972; Hans Kung, *On Being a Christian* 1978 chap Bi; ed.A.E.Harvey, *God Incarnate; story & belief* 1981.
2. Matt 16.16; Mark 8.29; Luke 9.20.
3. Acts 2.22–24, 32, 33, 36.
4. Acts 5.30f.
5. eg in J.D.G.Dunn *Christology in the Making* 1980 and A.T.Hanson *The Image of the Invisible God* 1982.
6. eg John 1.1–18, 2 Peter 1.1–11.
7. The main section of the definition is given in English in *Creeds, Councils & Controversies* ed. J.Stevenson 1966, pp.334–337.

8. see D.M.Baillie *God was in Christ* 1948, p.90, note 2.
9. cf Frances Young in *The Myth of God Incarnate* p.25f.
10. eg E.L.Mascall *Theology & the Gospel of Christ* 1977, part 3.
11. *Christus Veritas* p.142f quoted in N.Anderson *The Mystery of the Incarnation* 1978, p.134.
12. P.Schoonenberg, *The Christ* 1972, p.82.
13. *ibid.* p.86, note 17.
14. *ibid.* p.89f.
15. Athanasius *On the Incarnation* chap 54.3.
16. P.Tillich *Systematic Theology* 1968 vol 1. p.263.
17. J.Macquarrie *Principles of Christian Theology* 2nd rev. ed chap 5.
18. The first sentence of R.E.C.Browne *The Ministry of the Word* 1958.
19. P.Tillich *Systematic Theology* Vol 2, p.114.
20. J.Macquarrie *op cit* p.271.
21. *ibid.* p.302.
22. John Newton's hymn 'How sweet the name of Jesus sounds' (English Hymnal No 405 verse 4)
23. cf W.Pannenberg *Jesus, God and Man* 1968 pp.212ff.
24. D.M.Baillie *op cit* chap 5.
25. J.MacIntyre *The Shape of Christology* 1966, p.130.

Part 3

1. cf. W.A.Curtis, *History of Creeds & Confessions of Faith*, 1911, chap 2.
2. J.N.D.Kelly, *Early Christian Creeds*, 1950, p.73.
3. See texts on pp. 134–136. Kelly, *op cit.* pp.91ff.
4. The *Quicunque Vult* is known traditionally as the Athanasian Creed; for further on this paragraph see Kelly, *op cit.* p. 348ff.
5. cf J.N.D.Kelly, *Early Christian Doctrines*, 1958, chap X.
6. Kelly, *Creeds*, pp.358ff.
7. A.E.Burn, *The Nicene Creed*, 1929, p.45.
8. St Augustine, Sermon 58, quoted Curtis, *op cit.* p.xx.
9. *De Trin.* ii,1,2, quoted Burn, *op cit.* p.18.
10. *De Trin.* v,10.
11. Bishop J.Pearson, *An Exposition of the Creed*, 1659, on 'I believe etc.'
12. Jeremy Taylor, *A Discourse on the Liberty of Prophesying*, 1647, Section II on Heresy.
13. The Doctrine Commission of the Church of England, *Believing in the Church*, 1981, pp.125ff.

14. E.J.Bicknell, *A Theological Introduction to the Thirty-Nine Articles*, 1925, p.25.
15. Curtis, *op cit.* p.430.
16. Owen Chadwick, *Hensley Henson*, 1983, pp.35ff.
17. Roger Lloyd, *The Church of England in the Twentieth Century*, 1946, Vol 1, p.87.
18. George Bell, *Randall Davidson*, 1935, Vol 1, pp.395ff.
19. R.Lloyd, *op cit.* pp.96ff.
20. G.Bell, *op cit.* chap LIII.
21. *Doctrine in the Church of England*, 1938, pp.37–38.
22. *Doctrine in the Church of England*, 1938, pp.38–39.
23. Archbishops' Commission on Christian Doctrine, *Subscription & Assent to the Thirty-Nine Articles*, 1968.
24. in J.C.Satge, J.I.Packer, H.G.G.Herklots, G.W.H.Lampe & H.E.W.Turner, *The Articles of the Church of England*, 1964.
25. *Believing in the Church*, 1981, p.134.
26. An important step towards making it universal is whenever in the Western Church the Nicene Creed is recited without the *Filioque* clause; this does not deny the doctrine of the double procession but rather affirms the importance of keeping the text of an historic confession intact.
27. A.Tilby, *Won't you join the dance?*, 1985, cf p.1.
28. John Macquarrie, *Principles of Christian Theology*, 1966 & 1977, p.181.

Select Bibliography

The Virgin Birth, Nature Miracles & Resurrection of Jesus

Bishops of the Church of England The Nature of Christian Belief Church House Publishing, London, 1986

Brown,R.E. *The Virginal Conception and Bodily Resurrection of Jesus* Chapman, London 1973

Brown,R.E. *The Birth of the Messiah* Chapman, London, 1977

Fuller,R.H. *Interpreting the Miracles* SCM, London, 1977

Hendrickx,H. *The Infancy Narratives* Chapman, London, 1984

Hendrickx,H. *The Resurrection Narratives* Chapman, London, 1984

Jenkins,D.E. *God, Miracle and the Church of England* SCM, London, 1987ed.

Keller,E. & M.L, *Miracles in Dispute* SCM, London, 1969

Marxsen,W. *The Resurrection of Jesus of Nazareth* SCM, London, 1970

Moule,C.F.D. *Miracles* Mowbray, London & Oxford, 1965

Perkins,P. *Resurrection* Chapman, London, 1984

Robinson,J.A.T. *The Human Face of God* SCM, London, 1972

van Daalen,D.H. *The Real Resurrection* Collins, London, 1972

Wilkens U. *Resurrection* T&T Clark, Edinburgh, 1977

Christology

Baker,J.A. *The Foolishness of God* (Part Two) Darton, Longman and Todd, London, 1970

Hanson,A.T. *Grace and Truth* SPCK, London, 1975

ed.Harvey,A.E. *God Incarnate; Story & Belief* SPCK, London, 1981

Knox,J. *The Humanity and Divinity of Christ* C.U.P., Cambridge, 1967

Mackey,J.P. *Jesus, the Man and the Myth* SCM, London, 1979

Mackey,J.P. *The Christian Experience of God as Trinity* SCM, London, 1983

Marshall,H. *The Origins of New Testament Christology* Inter-Varsity Press, Leicester, 1976

Moule,C.F.D. *The Origin of Christology* C.U.P. Cambridge, 1977

Robinson,J.A.T. *The Human Face of God* SCM, London, 1972

Schoonenberg,P.*The Christ* Sheed & Ward, London 1969

ed. Sykes, S.W. & Clayton, J.P. *Christ, Faith & History* C.U.P. Cambridge, 1972

Turner, H.E.W. *Jesus the Christ* Mowbrays, London & Oxford, 1976

Creeds

Davies,R.E. *Making Sense of the Creeds* Epworth, London, 1987

Doctrine Commission of the C of E *Christian Believing* SPCK, London 1976

Doctrine Commission of the C of E *Believing in the Church* SPCK. London, 1981

Edwards,D.L. *Religion and Change* Hodder, London 1969

Dyson,A. *We believe* Mowbrays, London & Oxford, 1977

Kelly,J.N.D. *Early Christian Creeds* Longmans, London, 1950

Macquarrie, J. *Principles of Christian Theology* SCM, London, Rev. Ed 1977

Wainwright, G. *Doxology* Epworth, London, 1980

Young,F.M.*From Nicaea to Chalcedon* SCM, London, 1983